sew me!

sew and go

sew me!

sew and go

Easy-to-Make Totes, Tech Covers & Other Carry-Alls

Choly Knight

Design Originals

an Imprint of Fox Chapel Publishing
www.d-originals.com

ACQUISITION EDITOR
Peg Couch

COPY EDITOR
Colleen Dorsey

COVER AND PAGE DESIGNERS
Lindsay Hess, Ashley Millhouse

COVER AND PROJECT PHOTOGRAPHER
Scott Kriner

EDITOR
Katie Weeber

LAYOUT DESIGNER
Maura J. Zimmer

STEP-BY-STEP PHOTOGRAPHER
Matthew McClure

ISBN 978-1-57421-506-9

Library of Congress Cataloging-in-Publication Data

Knight, Choly.
  Sew me! sew and go : easy-to-make totes, tech covers, and other carry-alls / Choly Knight.
    pages cm
  Includes index.
  ISBN 978-1-57421-506-9
  1. Sewing. 2. Tote bags. 3. Containers. I. Title. II. Title: Sew and go.
  TT667.K589 2015
  646.4'8--dc23
                    2013047491

© 2015 by Choly Knight and New Design Originals Corporation, www.d-originals.com, an imprint of Fox Chapel Publishing, 800-457-9112, 1970 Broad Street, East Petersburg, PA 17520.

Printed in China
First printing

About the Author

Choly Knight is from Orlando, Florida, and is the author of *Sew Kawaii!*, *Sew Baby*, *Sewing Stylish Handbags & Totes*, *Sew Me! Sewing Basics*, and *Sew Me! Sewing Home Décor*. She has been crafting for as long as she can remember, and has drawn, painted, sculpted, and stitched everything in sight. She began sewing clothing in 1997 and has yet to put her sewing machine away. After studying studio art and earning a BA in English, she now enjoys trying to find numerous different ways to combine her passions for writing, fine art, and craft art. She created all of the designs, projects, and patterns that appear in this book. She focuses on handcrafted clothing, accessories, and other creations inspired by Japanese art, anime, and style, and specializes in cosplay (costume play) hats and hoodies. You can find out more about her and her work on her website: *www.cholyknight.com*.

Author Choly Knight

Contents

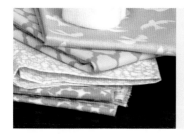

Make On-the-Go Accessories!

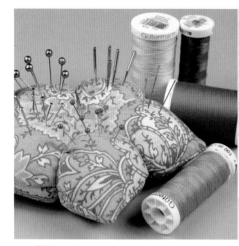

25 Build your basic sewing kit.

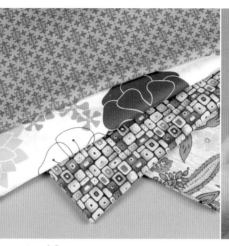

14 Select the perfect fabric for each project.

22 Learn how to laminate items and fuse plastic bags to create your own unique sewable fabric.

30 Refresh your memory on the basic techniques.

30 Review the standard machine stitches.

35 Get tips for working with tricky knit fabrics.

41 Understand how to work with patterns.

37 Learn how to enhance a project with appliqué.

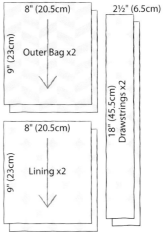

8" (20.5cm)   2½" (6.5cm)

9" (23cm) Outer Bag x2

18" (45.5cm) Drawstrings x2

8" (20.5cm)

9" (23cm) Lining x2

46 Discover charts and diagrams to walk you through the prep work.

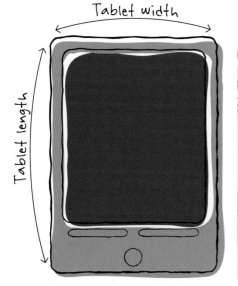

Tablet width

Tablet length

58 Take measurements to create projects that fit your exact needs.

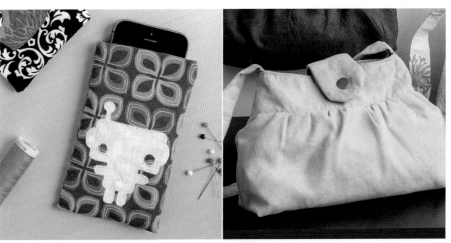

46 Start with simple, quick projects.

88 Tackle ambitious projects as your skills improve!

Introduction

If you've picked up this book, then something about sewing accessories for yourself has gotten you excited. Maybe you dream of making fashionable bags worthy of the catwalk, want to personalize your electronic devices with cases in creative colors and prints, have a new sewing machine and want to know how to make it work for you, or simply want to treat yourself and those closest to you to handmade treasures. But with all those lofty ideas in the future, it can seem daunting to take that first step and get going.

I, too, was intimidated by the daunting task of threading the needle. It's hard not to feel scared when setting out to sew your own personal accessories for the first time. What finally convinced me it was worthwhile was my first Home Economics class in middle school. Seeing how a few simple yards of cotton could be transformed into a useful item made me realize the limitless possibilities of sewing. The machine, shears, and needles were only tools—I just had to find out what made them tick and they were mine to control, not to fear.

I know you will feel the same way when you discover all the techniques and tools you can use to create beautiful accessories that perfectly suit your personal taste. Appliqué, zippers, buttons, and interfacing are like paints on your palette, ready to be used on the canvas. And you really can't beat the feeling of making something from nothing—taking plain fabric and turning it into something useful and beautiful with just your two hands and a sewing machine. Soon, you'll begin to see raw materials in a whole new light. An old button-down shirt can become a clever purse front or book cover; old scraps of fabric can be sewn into a handy case for your cell phone. Your whole perspective will change when you begin to see the opportunities.

Despite the kind of creativity you can feel while sewing, people often ask me why I bother. Why go through the trouble of sewing when extremely cheap accessories can be found just about anywhere? It's true, the cheapest bag or electronic case on the market can't compare with the cost of sewing for yourself, but there are lots of other reasons to take sewing into your own hands.

Everyone can use a cute little case or a book strap to hold items used throughout the day. But the cases and straps you find in the store will never have the same personality and versatility as ones you make yourself. Both of these items can be customized to the exact size you want, with colors you love and appliqué you adore!

After I got a taste of thread and fabric, I realized I didn't have to settle any longer. It's strangely perfect that I learned to sew when I did, because I was already excited about developing my own sense of taste, style, and individuality. Sewing helped me unlock those things to their full potential. While shopping for a bag to match my favorite outfit, I could (almost defiantly) say that, no, I didn't like this season's colors! And no, I wasn't going to put my tablet in a generic plastic case. I would just make one of my own!

Over the years, I developed a very specific taste that could only be satisfied by intense and arduous retail shopping trips or a single, easy trip to the fabric store. My history with arts and crafts makes my taste a little quirky, and I find I'm always disappointed by the selection of goods at everyday stores. Sewing is how I know I can get exactly what I want—that I can make a chic purse that matches my favorite outfit perfectly, or an organizer that can hold every device I carry snugly and safely. I encourage all of you would-be sewers out there with an eccentric or particular sense of style to pick up your needles, if only for this reason. In the end, making things yourself ensures your accessories will be truly unique, and you've probably paid much less for that custom look!

This brings us back the original argument: is sewing really cheaper than buying? For bargain-basement wares like grocery totes, pencil cases, etc., buying can often be the less expensive option. Basics that wear out after a year of use are nearly impossible to beat pricewise, but suppose you want something more high-end? A polished purse or a grown-up pencil case for art supplies? You'll see the store prices jump for these items, though the quality of materials and construction might be exactly the same as their cheaper counterparts. If you shop for the right fabrics at the right time, you can easily purchase exactly what you need for half the price of the finished product at a department store.

Not having to pay someone else for labor is the boon here. If you're making it yourself, you'll know the construction is much better than what you would get from a factory that rushes hundreds of units a day, so your project will last longer too! It's true, the cost of tools and notions is pricey at first, but if you keep sewing, then the investment in tools you'll use for years will save you more and more money in the long run.

With all of this in mind, you'll learn that sewing doesn't have to be scary, restricting, or expensive. You can see how your tools will work for you to achieve whatever you can imagine, whether it's unique, creative, or frugal. Yes, there will be headaches and there will be mistakes, but if you're willing to try, you'll see at most they will result in some stitches to rip and a bit of fabric wasted. No amount of frustration can compare with the feeling of creating your own one-of-a-kind pieces, and this book will help take you on that fabulous journey!

Sewing gives you tons of options, like creating a reversible tote bag to carry all your stuff. Sewing this project yourself means you can pick colors to match your favorite outfit, or fabrics that are suited to your needs, like heavy canvas for trips to the grocery store, or terry cloth for a gym/shower bag.

Getting Started

The projects in this book require some very basic sewing techniques, so if you are familiar with sewing you can look through this section to refresh your memory about the basic skills you'll be using. If you're not so familiar with sewing, however, this chapter is great to get you acquainted with some indispensible information about skills, techniques, and fabrics. For more information, check out *Sew Me! Sewing Basics*.

This chapter will also give you information about the projects, which are ranked by difficulty, taking into account the time required and complexity of the techniques used. If you want to get the most out of this book, start with the very easy projects and work your way up. You'll find that as your skills increase, you'll be able to tackle more and more difficult projects until you have created personalized accessories to meet all your needs!

Fabrics

Purchasing fabric for a project is always an exciting process, and with a little bit of knowledge going in, you can ensure your trip to the fabric store is a creative adventure instead of an arduous process. Picking the right fabric can help you make a project you'll want to keep forever. Here's everything you need to know about finding and buying fabric so you're sure to be happy with your purchase.

The best way to categorize fabrics so you make the right choice is to divide them into fabrics that stretch and fabrics that don't. These are called wovens and knits. Beyond that, they are broken down by thickness or weight. If you learn to see fabric in this way, you'll be sure to get the best fabric for the job.

WOVEN FABRICS

Woven fabrics are the kind that should come to mind when you think of your favorite button-down shirt, a sturdy tote bag, or a fancy pair of slacks. These fabrics are made by weaving threads together, just like basket pieces, to form the fabric. They can be made from synthetic or natural fibers and range from large weaves like burlap to delicate weaves like fine silk.

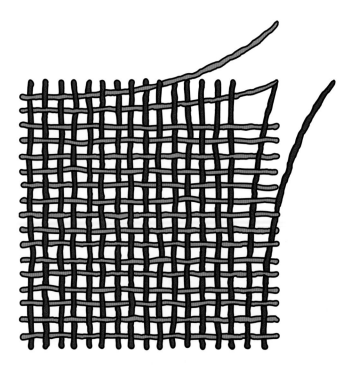

Wovens: Woven fabrics are made just like a basket, but on a much smaller scale. They're sturdy and reliable, but have the unfortunate quality of unraveling as the threads gradually pull away at the edges.

About Metric

Throughout this book, you'll notice that every measurement is accompanied by a metric equivalent. Inches and yards are rounded off to the nearest half or whole centimeter unless precision is necessary. Please be aware that while this book will show 1 yard = 100 centimeters, the actual conversion is 1 yard = 90 centimeters, a difference of about 3 15/16" (10cm). Using these conversions, you will always have a little bit of extra fabric if purchasing by the metric quantity.

Lightweight wovens

Lightweight woven fabrics encompass some very reliable and versatile fabrics that are perfect for beginners. Lightweight fabrics tend to bend and twist more easily and are more accommodating to your projects. If your project has curves, ruffles, or intricate shapes, stick with a lightweight fabric.

Quilting cotton: It doesn't get more reliable than quilting cotton. Although this fabric is meant for quilts, it can be used for accessories and clothing as well. In fact, just about every project in this book can be made from quilting cotton. It's sturdy, behaves predictably, irons beautifully, and is perfect for beginners. You can find it in a multitude of designs, and it gets softer with every wash. Solid varieties of this cotton are called broadcloth, and versions woven with a smooth, shiny finish are called sateen cotton.

Flannel: Flannel is like the softer cousin of quilting cotton. It's still just as reliable but has a slightly fuzzy, brushed feel to it.

Shirting: This is an umbrella term used to describe fabrics that work well for shirts. They are typically made from synthetic fibers or blends, and can range in texture from smooth like quilting cotton and fluffy like flannel to puckered textures like gauze, gingham, and seersucker. They sew similarly to cotton, except they are less stiff and therefore work better for shirts.

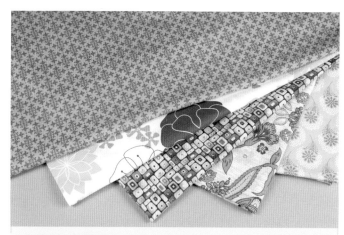

Quilting cotton

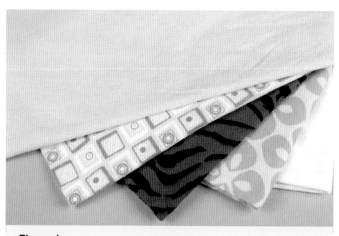

Flannel

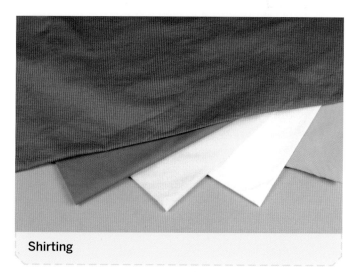

Shirting

Silk & satin: Satin and similar fabrics are typically made from synthetic fibers and have a quality that's often called "slinky" or "drapey." If you pinch the middle of the fabric and hold it up, you'll see that the surrounding fabric drapes completely with almost no stiffness. This drapey quality, in addition to the beautiful sheen, is what makes satin such a luxury. Unfortunately, this is also what makes satin move so unpredictably while you sew. It takes a bit of practice to get used to satin, so start out with small projects after you've honed your skills with more stable fabrics.

Medium-weight wovens

Medium-weight fabrics can't conform to as many shapes and details as light-weight fabrics, but they make up for it by being heftier and great for taking on tougher tasks.

Linen: Linen is a similar fabric to cotton, being very easy to work with and reliable. It's made from a natural fiber (flax), though synthetic blends are very common and can change the feel of the fabric. It's associated with the noticeable woven fibers that run through it, and it often has a drapey quality.

Twill & denim: Twill is a kind of woven fabric that is defined by the diagonal weave present in the fabric texture (so denim is a kind of twill). However, it can best be described as the fabric used for khaki pants or light jackets. It is often made from cotton, although stretchable synthetics and blends are common. It sews very predictably, though its thickness makes it a little less forgiving. Fabrics similar to twill are often found with the name bottomweights.

Silk & satin

Linen

Twill

Corduroy: Corduroy is a fabric similar to twill that has raised "cords" with a velvet-like texture. It sews up nicely, although care must be taken that the cords run in the right direction in the finished product. This is called the nap, and means the direction where stroking the fabric feels smooth and natural (like an animal's coat). Various prints and colors are becoming popular with this fabric, making it great for bags and cases.

Brocade: Brocade is a kind of satin with layers of embroidery in the woven fabric. It's much more stable than its thinner cousins, so although sewing with satin can be tricky, brocades can be rather kind to beginners by comparison. Besides that, it's hard to turn down all those gorgeous colors and patterns.

Suiting: Suiting fabric is a bit of an umbrella term to cover fabrics that work well for making suits. They're typically made from combinations of wool, polyester, and rayon and come in sophisticated and classic colors and prints.

Corduroy

Brocade

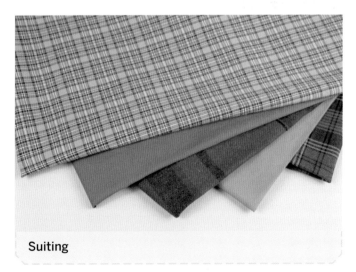

Suiting

Heavyweight wovens

The average person typically encounters heavyweight fabrics through furniture and home textiles. Fabrics like these work better on a large scale, or if not that, at least with straight, simple lines with few curves and corners. So while heavyweight fabrics are typically harder to work with, here are some suggestions that should encourage you to experiment.

Canvas: Typically made from cotton or linen, canvas is a thick fabric with a very large weave. It tends to be stiff and difficult to sew through, but with the right sewing needle, the results are strong and sturdy. It is also known as cotton duck.

Home décor fabrics: This is an umbrella term that covers various thick and printed varieties of fabrics for window dressings and upholstery. Smooth solid and printed varieties of twill and canvas work nicely for totes and book covers. However, heavily embroidered and plush varieties can overcomplicate your project and make sewing difficult, so steer clear of those until you've had more practice with simpler fabrics.

Faux suede: This fabric is a bit of a guilty pleasure for me, and I snatch it up whenever I find it. The texture is wonderful and the range of colors available is amazing. This suede substitute is made from adhering a suede-like nap onto a woven fabric. It sews very well, though ironing can sometimes damage the surface. At stores it might also be called suedecloth or ultrasuede.

Heavyweight fabrics: Fabrics like canvas, simple home décor fabrics, and faux suede are great heavyweights for beginners.

KNIT FABRICS

Knit fabrics are constructed differently from woven fabrics in that they are created by knitting threads to form the fabric. This is similar to the way a sweater is made (but on a much smaller scale) and exactly what you find in your favorite t-shirts. Knit fabrics are special in that they stretch, usually horizontally along the fabric, but sometimes both horizontally and vertically. Because of this, knits are typically used for clothing and wearable accessories because they conform to the shape of the body. It is challenging to make accessories like bags and cases from knits due to the stretchy nature of the fabric, but it can be done! If you've found a knit fabric you simply must have, try applying some sturdy interfacing to the wrong side before you sew it, and use a woven lining. Your finished project will have a cozy, slouchy feel like a hand-knitted purse! If your knit fabrics still stretch a bit after the interfacing is applied, check out the tips on page 35 to ensure your success.

Lightweight knits

Jersey: This is the name to look for when you consider a thin t-shirt fabric. It's manufactured with a right side (the flat, or knit side if you are a knitter) and a wrong side (the piled or purl side). It is extremely stretchy along the horizontal axis, which can make it tricky to sew, but results in a very lovely drape. It comes in cotton and synthetic blends and is sometimes called single knit.

Lycra & spandex: These fabrics are similar to jersey in their weight, yet they are made from synthetic materials like polyester, nylon, rayon, and Lycra. They sometimes stretch in four directions, making fit easier. This is what's used to make swimsuits and leotards, so fusing a sturdy interfacing to your fabric if you want to use it to make accessories is all the more important.

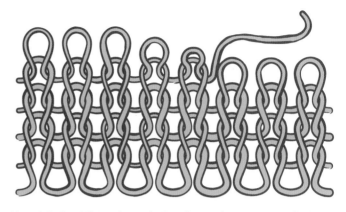

Knit fabrics: Threads are knitted together to create knit fabrics, which have the wonderful quality of stretching to fit snugly but not unraveling.

Jersey

Lycra & spandex

Medium-weight knits

Interlock: Like jersey, this fabric is knitted, but it is knitted in two layers so both sides are finished to look smooth. Because the fabric is thicker, it doesn't stretch nearly as much, so there's less drape, but it's also somewhat easier to work with. This fabric comes in a great abundance of natural fibers and synthetic blends.

Fleece: Fleece is a polyester fabric with a soft nap knitted into the base of the textile. This popular fabric can be seen in a lot of store-bought jackets, hats, and mittens and sews very easily for beginners. While it stretches enough to fit well, the stretchiness doesn't affect how it sews, so I can't recommend it enough for all your warm and fluffy projects. It's also available in a plethora of solid colors and prints.

Minky: Minky is a kind of faux fur similar in construction to fleece. The feel, however, is remarkably soft and delightful. It comes in lots of bright colors and piles, from short and smooth to shaggy and long to novelty designs like diamonds and stripes.

Interlock

Fleece

Minky

ADDITIONAL OPTIONS

Felt: Set slightly apart from other fabrics, felt is typically thought of more for crafting and accessories. Its fibers are neither woven nor knit, but rather intensely compressed to form a sheet. Because of this, using high-quality woolen felt is always best, as the fibers will be less likely to separate over time. And because felt does not fray, it is perfect for tiny embellishments and details such as appliqué.

Terry cloth: Terry cloth is a fabric that really works double time. Many new varieties are extremely soft and colorful. Cut-up towels work beautifully as a substitute, and using a bit of terry cloth for appliqué or other small touches can transform your favorite case or bag into one for the beach, gym, or bathroom!

Vinyl & faux leather: Vinyl and faux leather are heavyweight fabrics that act more like plastic. They have great strength and durability, but are often difficult to work with because they don't run through the machine easily. A lightweight stabilizer can help with this; see the Sewing Tools section (page 25) for more information. Also be sure to use a sewing machine needle made specifically for vinyl or leather when sewing with these fabrics.

Felt

Terry cloth

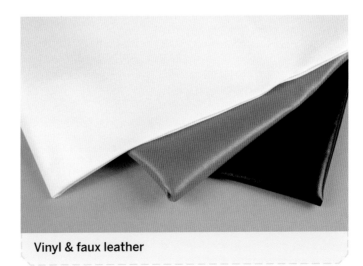

Vinyl & faux leather

Recycled materials: See below for information on how to melt and reuse plastic bags for sewing and also how to laminate items with iron-on vinyl for sewing. Anything from grocery bags, food bags, old books, artwork, and even gift-wrapping paper will work! These materials will act very similarly to vinyl and faux leather and will require a needle for vinyl to sew properly.

Found fabrics: You'll find a great resource for project supplies at thrift stores or anywhere else used items are sold. Old pants or jackets make for wonderfully sturdy fabric and old dresses are nice for lining or creating a fancier look. Even better are the bits of old hardware you can find on old bags and luggage.

Recycled materials

Found fabrics

FUSING PLASTIC BAGS INTO SEWABLE FABRIC

Grocery store bags only ever seem to have one or two uses in them before they start falling apart. Why not make them more durable by fusing several bags together into a thick sheet? This sheet is then sewable, and you can use it to make any number of projects. To make one sheet, gather up about three to four grocery bags and large sheets of parchment paper. Also make sure to open your windows and get plenty of ventilation in case some unwelcome fumes start to come off the plastic.

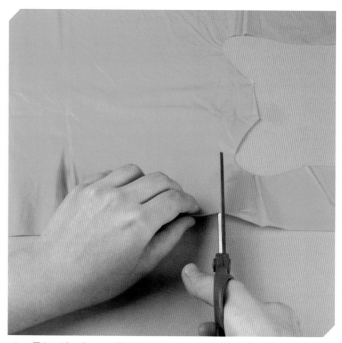

1 **Trim the bags.** Flatten and smooth out the bags, and then trim off the handles and bottom seam. You should be left with a smooth sheet of plastic that forms a tube.

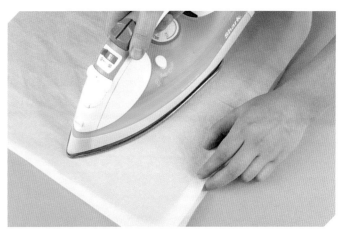

2 **Layer the plastic between the paper.** Layer the tube of plastic between the sheets of parchment paper. If your bag has writing on it, turn it inside out so the ink doesn't melt onto the parchment paper.

3 **Iron the plastic.** Using a medium-low setting on the iron and with the steam turned off, iron over the sheet of parchment paper to meld the plastic together. Run the iron smoothly and evenly over the paper for about thirty seconds until the pieces are fused.

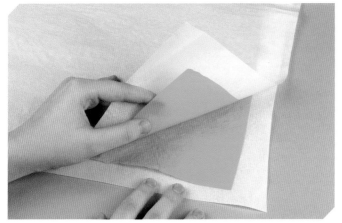

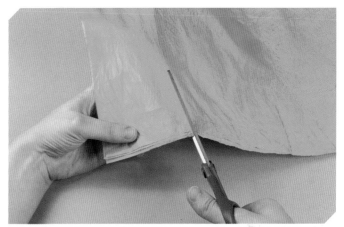

4 **Add more plastic.** Allow the plastic to cool completely and peel the parchment paper off. Add more sheets of plastic and repeat Step 3 until you have a 6-ply sheet. An 8-ply sheet would also work well if your bags are especially thin or you want a stronger, thicker project.

5 **Finish and use the sheet.** After several repetitions of Step 3, you'll have a sturdy sheet of plastic that is ready to sew. You can cut it with scissors or a craft knife to the shape you need, and it won't unravel like fabric. Be sure to use a needle intended for vinyl when sewing with it.

Not all plastic is created equal

Each plastic bag can be different, so it helps to experiment first when ironing your bags. Use the scraps from the handles if necessary to see how your plastic reacts to different heat settings. When fusing the bags, there's a sweet spot that is the goal. The plastic should get hot enough to melt, but not so hot that it warps, shrinks, or forms holes. Experiment with different heat settings and how fast you move the iron.

When you check your fused plastic, shallow wrinkles are completely normal. However, deep wrinkles are a sign that the iron may have been too hot, so try to go cooler next time. Bubbles are a sign that the plastic didn't get hot enough to fuse completely. These can be weak points and should be ironed again.

LAMINATING MEDIA WITH IRON-ON VINYL

In addition to melting plastic bags, you can make your own vinyl fabric from collected media and iron-on vinyl. Gather up any interesting flat media like food wrappers, photos, newspapers, or even items you've collaged yourself, and laminate them with iron-on vinyl. The result can be used to make any project that is suitable for vinyl and faux leather—all with fabric you designed!

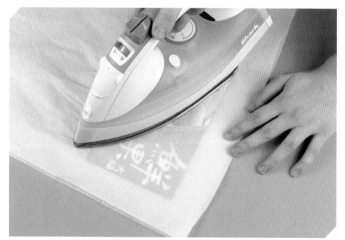

1 **Prepare the medium.** Prepare the item you wish to laminate by making sure it is trimmed of unwanted parts and is entirely smooth, flat, and clean. Lay it on a larger piece of parchment paper.

2 **Layer the sheets.** Apply the adhesive side of the iron-on vinyl to the right side of your medium. Sandwich this between two sheets of parchment paper.

3 **Iron the vinyl.** Iron the vinyl to the medium following the manufacturer's instructions. After cooling, the vinyl should be completely adhered to the medium. Repeat Steps 2–3 for the other side of the medium.

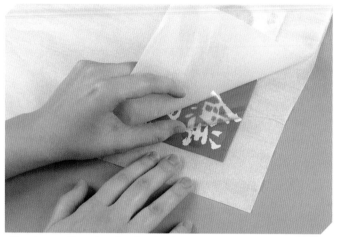

4 **Prepare the piece for sewing.** Trim away the excess vinyl and use the piece to cut out your pattern. It can be cut with scissors or a craft knife and sewn with a needle suitable for vinyl or faux leather.

Sewing Tools

You can get through just about any project in this book with the most basic sewing tools one would usually have in a sewing kit. Some other, more specialty, tools are useful to have to make the process easier and quicker, so look through them here if you feel like you want to add them to your arsenal.

BASIC SEWING KIT

Sewing machine: Check out the book *Sew Me! Sewing Basics* to learn how to buy and what to look for in a great sewing machine that you can rely on for years to come.

Sewing shears: Unlike regular scissors, sewing shears are much sharper and, when taken care of properly, can cut through fabric like butter. Avoid cutting paper with them because this will dull the blades quickly.

You don't have to go expensive to get the job done, but the more expensive, higher-quality shears can last a lifetime (with sharpening) and are ideal if you want to sew further down the line.

Craft scissors: A typical pair of comfortable scissors work fine as craft scissors. Use these to cut paper patterns, thread, or any other material that would dull sewing shears.

Sewing shears are essential for every sewing project. Large sewing shears are best for cutting large pieces of fabric down to the appropriate dimensions, but you can also purchase medium and small shears for trimming smaller pieces of fabric and thread. Always take good care of your sewing shears and they'll stay sharp through many projects. Even an inexpensive pair will cut much better than anything in your junk drawer.

Tape measure or ruler: Sewing doesn't have to be an exact science, but it's good to have a ruler around so you know you are accurately making your project to the size you want. A tape measure is a necessity when sewing clothes or other large projects. You'll want the flexible fabric kind; they're extremely cheap, so it doesn't hurt to have more than one if the sewing bug has really bit you. For rulers, a yardstick often does the trick, but if you're willing to spend the extra money on a transparent quilting ruler you'll find it's very helpful for cutting pattern pieces.

Seam ripper: This strange-looking tool is for picking out and cutting stitches in seams you'd like to undo. Even the best of us make mistakes, so don't be afraid to use one.

Iron: Ironing is really crucial for professional-looking results in projects made with crisp fabrics such as cotton, twill, and the like. Even a cheap iron can do the job, but more expensive irons are a good investment if you plan to sew for years. Higher-quality irons are heavier (to make pressing and creasing easier), have more precise heat settings, and also have steam and spray functions.

Fabric marker: If there's one little tool that will save you from sewing headaches, it has to be the fabric marker. These pens are made with disappearing (or water-soluble) ink that can be used to draw on your fabric. You can use these to mark places for buttons, zippers, pockets, or anything else that needs to be matched up on your main fabric. You might think it's unnecessary, but you'd be surprised how a little mark can go a long way. Consider getting a light-colored pencil for dark fabrics and a dark marker for light fabrics.

Carbon tracing paper & wheel: An alternative to fabric markers is carbon tracing paper and a tracing wheel. First, the carbon paper and fabric are stacked, and then the wheel is run along the pattern guidelines. This transfers carbon marks to the fabric, which can be washed away later.

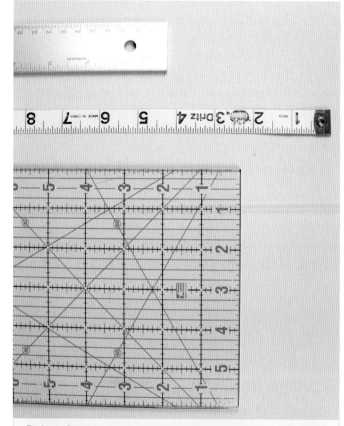

Rulers & tape measures: You'll need these to measure accurate cuts in your fabric.

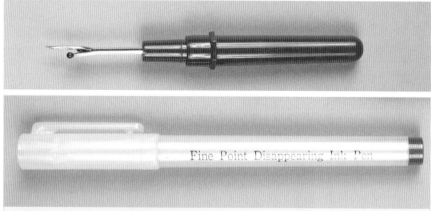

Seam ripper & fabric marker: Little tools that make a world of difference!

Sewing pins: These little guys are used to temporarily hold pieces of fabric together while you sew. They come in different lengths and degrees of sharpness, but beginners should be more comfortable with larger, longer pins with big plastic heads. They sometimes leave slightly noticeable holes in your fabric, but you can work your way up to smaller, less obtrusive pins as you get comfortable.

Sewing machine needle: Your sewing machine needs a special kind of needle that fits specifically into your machine. They are made to suit different thicknesses of fabric in both knit and woven varieties. They are assigned a number between 8 and 19 (American) or 60 and 120 (European), with the low numbers in the range for light fabrics and the higher numbers for heavier fabrics. Specialty needles take care of leather or metallic embroidery. The best thing to do if you are confused is to read the package, which usually describes what the needle is for. Universal needles, around size 10–11, are perfect for beginners, but if you're venturing out into new fabric realms, try to find a needle that matches your selection the best.

Hand-sewing needles: There are specific needles for hand sewing, and these are called "sharps." They come in a range of sizes, though as the needles get larger, they are usually labeled for embroidery and tapestry sewing. Find a size that feels comfortable for you within the sharps range.

Thread: Thread is the glue that's going to hold all your projects together, so it's good to get acquainted with it. While there are quite a few different forms of thread out there, be sure to look for all-purpose thread. This is a polyester blend of thread that works wonderfully for everything. Shiny rayon threads are meant for embroidery and all cotton threads for hand quilting, which isn't what we need here for sewing accessory projects. You will want to pick a thread that matches your fabric so contrasting colors don't peek out of your project. To see if your thread matches your fabric, hold a length of the thread across the fabric and see if it blends in. If you can't find the perfect color, go with a shade darker rather than lighter.

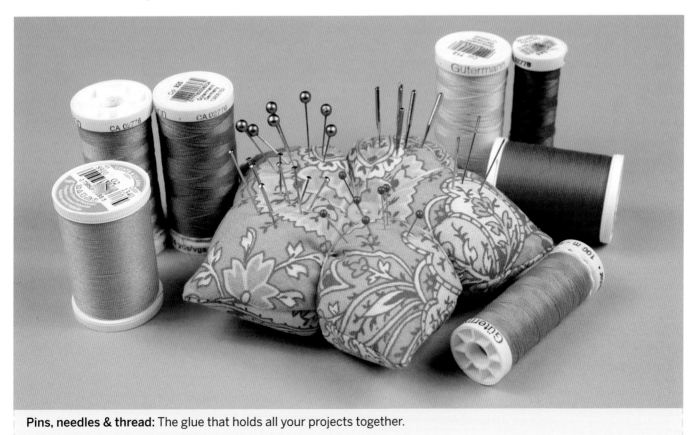

Pins, needles & thread: The glue that holds all your projects together.

Additional Supplies

In addition to basic tools and fabric, some projects call for special supplies. Some are called notions, others embellishments, but all are quite standard, easy to find, and helpful to keep around for other projects in the future.

Rotary cutter: Working much like a pizza cutter, a rotary cutter is a sharp-bladed tool that can cut long straight lines in a snap. It's a boon for quilting, and works best with a ruler to keep cuts straight and a mat underneath to protect surfaces from the sharp blade.

Pinking shears: Woven fabrics like cotton and flannel tend to unravel when their edges are left raw. A fast way of finishing those edges is with pinking shears, which cut the fabric in a zigzag pattern and prevent the edges from fraying to bits.

Ribbon: Ribbon is not only adorable for embellishment, but also has practical uses such as for closures or creating gathers. It comes in many widths and colors, so it can add a distinctive look to your project.

Bias tape: Made from cloth fabric cut on the bias (for a slight, but smooth, stretch), bias tape comes in many colors and is used to bind raw edges of fabrics quickly and easily. When the folded fabric is opened, it fits snugly over the raw edge and is sewn down.

Hook-and-loop tape: Hook-and-loop tape is a simple kind of closure that's great for beginners because it doesn't require any fiddling with buttons, zippers, or snaps. Go with the sew-on variety to make sure it stays in place.

Webbing, ribbon & bias tape: These notions are useful for both looks and utilitarian purposes.

More advanced cutting tools. Pinking shears and rotary cutters are a bit above and beyond basic sewing tools, but using them can save you hours of time if you're willing to make the investment.

Elastic: Standard elastic can be used to create gathers in fabric or cinch in roomy pockets. The more decorative varieties can be used on the outside of projects like wearables to add a unique touch.

Batting: Polyester batting is a definite go-to filling for plush items like pillows. You can also choose from the other fillings, such as micro pellets.

Quilt batting: This long and thin sheet of batting is made specifically for quilts. The polyester varieties are much fluffier, while the cotton varieties are thinner and denser. They typically come in packages for a specific blanket size or by the yard.

Beeswax: While not absolutely necessary for most projects, beeswax is useful for adding strength to thread for hand sewing. Running thread along a beeswax block coats it and prevents breaking and knots. The real advantage of strengthening the thread is to create long-lasting seams for your projects.

Interfacing: This material is used for stabilizing and giving greater support to fabric. It comes in iron- and sew-on varieties, as well as various weights. When attached to your fabric, it will make the fabric more stable and rigid. This is perfect if you want to use a lightweight fabric for a project that would normally require a heavyweight fabric, or to eliminate any stretching that your fabric might have. Interfacing also helps your projects keep their shape when you want them to have a particular look. Interfacing is sold by the yard or in precut packages. The majority of interfacing comes in 22" (56cm)-wide widths, so the projects in this book will reflect that when listing required materials.

Fusible fleece: Similar to interfacing is fusible fleece. It is a fiber that adheres to your fabric, just like interfacing, but provides cushion as well as support. Your fabric will be rigid and keep its shape, but also be slightly padded. In addition, there are also insulated varieties. Fusible fleece also comes by the yard or in precut packages. Most fusible and insulated fleece comes in 22" (56cm)-wide widths, so the projects in this book will reflect that when listing required materials.

Fusible web: Used in this book for appliqué, fusible web is a paper-backed adhesive that is adhered to your selected fabric with an iron. After peeling the paper away, the adhesive is left behind and can then be ironed to another surface. The lightweight variety is for appliqué that will be stitched, while the heavyweight

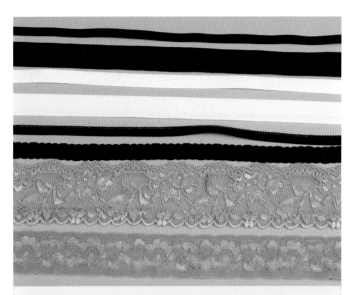

Varieties of elastic: Strong (but plain) bands of elastic are primarily used for their tough and stretchy qualities, while lacey decorative elastic is more delicate and cannot stand up to as much pulling.

Interfacing & fusible fleece: Interfacing adds stability to fabrics and comes in light-, medium-, and heavyweight varieties. Other special interfacings are fusible fleece and insulated fleece.

variety is for embellishments that aren't meant to be sewn, making it better for projects that won't get a lot of wear and tear. Fusible web is sold by the yard and in packages. See how fusible web is used in the appliqué feature (page 37).

Stabilizer: Stabilizer is often used in tandem with fusible web for the appliqué process. The dense stitches used for appliqué can often warp or put strain on fabric. Stabilizer prevents that from happening. Light- to medium-weight stabilizer is best for these projects, because the leftover margins can be torn away after use.

Sewing Techniques and Terms

Phrases and terms such as these might pop up in the directions for your project, and if you don't know what they mean, this is a good place to start to get the jargon cleared up.

MACHINE STITCHES

Basic stitch:
Width: 0
Length: Short to medium
This stitch is ideal for all of your general seaming needs. Go shorter for lighter, more delicate fabrics, and a bit longer for thicker, sturdier fabrics.

Basting and gathering stitch:
Width: 0
Length: Long
A straight stitch at maximum length is used for basting. This is a seam that's meant to hold fabric temporarily in place where it can't be seen or will be removed later. This is also used for gathering fabric to make items like ruffles. Learn more about that on page 34.

Buttonhole stitch:
Width: Narrow
Length: Short
A narrow and short zigzag stitch is what's used when making a buttonhole. Most machines come equipped with a feature to do this automatically, but if yours doesn't, it can be made freehand with this stitch.

Stretch stitch:
Width: Narrow
Length: Medium to long
A narrow zigzag with a longer length is used as a basic stretch stitch. When sewing knit fabrics, your finished seams will stretch along with the fabric when sewn with these stitches.

Appliqué zigzag stitch:
Width: Medium to wide
Length: Short
A medium to wide zigzag done in a short length makes a great stitch for sewing appliqué fabric. Turn to the appliqué feature (page 37) to see it in action.

Finishing stitch:
Width: Medium
Length: Medium to long
A basic zigzag stitch is perfect for finishing the edges of your fabric so they don't unravel. This can be done within the seam allowance or over the edge of the fabric.

Couching stitch:
Width: Wide
Length: Medium to long
Couching is a kind of decorative technique that sews down cords, yarn, or other embellishments to your fabric. This same technique can sew down a thin piece of ribbon or string that can be used to easily gather your fabric.

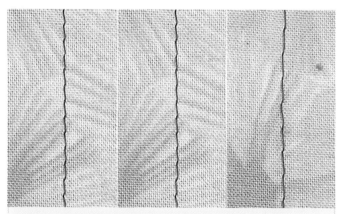

Straight stitches: Vary your stitch length to get short stitches suitable for fine fabrics, medium length stitches for light- to medium-weight fabrics, and long stitches for basting and gathering.

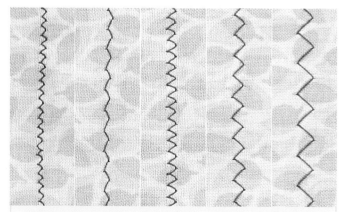

Zigzag stitches: Vary your stitch length and width to get stitches for buttonholes, knit fabrics, appliqué, finishing, and couching.

HAND SEWING

Just a bit of hand sewing practice can get you through the projects in this book. Here are the stitches that come up most frequently.

Make a knot at the tail ends of your thread, or make a knot in your fabric before you start stitching. Do this by weaving the needle through a small bit of fabric, around ⅛" (0.5cm), and then pull the thread until the tail ends stick out by about 1" (2.5cm). Repeat the same stitch in the same spot, but before you tighten the stitch, loop the needle through the loop in your thread, similar to a half-hitch knot.

Backstitch: This is the basic hand-sewing stitch used in place of a sewing machine stitch. After creating your knot in the thread or fabric, insert your needle into the beginning of the seam. Bring it up about ½" (1.5cm) away. Insert the needle again, going backward about ¼" (0.5cm), and then up ¼" (0.5cm) beyond the previous stitch. This is a constant "two steps forward, one step back" rhythm that creates a very neat, yet strong, seam.

Basting stitch: This is a simple hand-sewing stitch that replaces the basting stitches done by your machine. You'll have much more control and can hold your fabric together without the aid of sharp pins! If you plan to remove these stitches later, avoid making a knot in your thread or fabric. Instead leave a very long thread tail to keep your seam from unraveling. Insert your needle into the beginning of the seam, and weave it back and forth through the layers by about 1" (2.5cm) per stitch.

Ladder stitch: This stitch is also known as a slip stitch, because you are slipping the needle into the folds of fabric to bring two folded edges together. This results in a nearly invisible seam that can be done from the outside of your project.

Create a knot from the inside of your project so it doesn't show, and then begin by weaving the needle in and out of one fold in your fabric, making a stitch about ¼" (0.5cm) long. Move to the next side, progressing forward, and repeat the same stitch. Tighten the stitches lightly as you go along, and you'll see the ladder shape formed by the threads will disappear into the fabric.

Create a knot at the end in the fabric, and then insert the needle beside the knot and through the project, pulling it away from your seam. Clip the thread while you pull and the thread tail will disappear into the finished project.

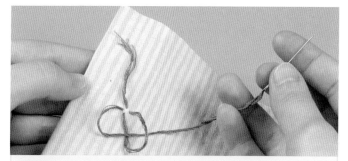

Knot your thread. Instead of creating a knot at the end of your thread, it's much more secure to create one tied into the fabric itself.

Backstitch: If you need to hand sew a seam that replaces a sewing machine stitch, the backstitch is the way to go.

Basting stitch: This stitch works well for temporary seams or for making ruffles as described on page 34.

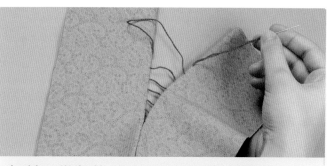

Ladder stitch: Also known as a slip stitch, this creates a nearly invisible seam from the outside of your project.

ADDITIONAL TERMS

Pattern symbols and guidelines: Pattern guidelines and symbols may differ, so it always helps to read over patterns and instructions before jumping into a project. The patterns from this book will list seam allowances, fold lines, seam lines, and grain lines. The circle symbols indicate where seams break and an opening is left, and gray lines show where to place appliqué or other project pieces. Mark these on your fabric using tracing paper or a fabric marker. The patterns will also indicate how many of each piece to cut, and in what color and fabric if it's helpful for the look of the project.

Seam allowance: This is the space between the edge of your fabric and where the seam is made. The standard for most U.S. patterns is ⅝" (1.5cm), though it can vary depending on the project and how small it is. Always check the pattern to know what your seam allowance is.

Grain line: The grain line of a fabric follows the direction in which the fabric was knitted or woven and goes parallel to the selvedge (the machine finished edges of the fabric). The pattern pieces have a grain line arrow that indicates how the pattern piece should be placed to ensure proper stretching and drape in the right directions.

Finishing edges: The raw edges of woven fabrics tend to unravel and fray apart if left unfinished. If you are using woven fabrics in your project, any exposed edges should be finished. This can be done with pinking shears, a zigzag stitch within the seam allowance, or with fray-blocking liquid.

Finishing edges. Certain fabrics can sometimes unravel when worked with or washed. Prevent this with pinking shears, a zigzag stitch, or fray-blocking liquid.

Clipping corners and curves: When sewing pieces that will be turned right-side out, the seam allowances of convex corners and curves should be clipped or trimmed to accommodate excess fabric when the shape is inverted. Alternately, the seam allowances of concave corners and curves should be clipped or trimmed to accommodate the fabric stretching when the shape is inverted.

Box stitch: This is done around the ends of straps or tabs attached to a project for added support and strength. The stitch is made by sewing a square around the end of the strap and then going diagonally across the square, creating an hourglass shape within the square. A single square without the X can be done for ease, but the X gives the greatest hold. Be sure to do lots of backstitching at the beginning and end of this seam for the greatest strength.

Topstitching: This is done for decorative and strength-increasing purposes for the outside of a project. Choose a thread that you are fine with being visible, and sew another seam about ¼" (0.5cm) from the previous seam. This creates a professional touch.

Clipping corners and curves. Seam allowances of curves and corners should be clipped before turning the pieces right side out.

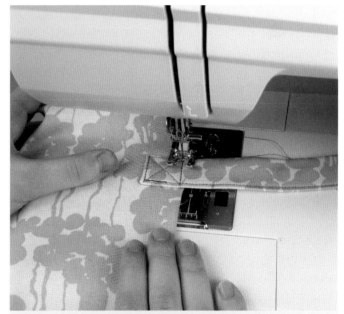

Box stitch. A box stitch is the go-to stitch for creating the most strength in a small space, so it's ideal for straps, hangers, and the like.

Hems: Single- and double-fold hems are the type of hems used for the projects in this book. These types of hems are done by folding the fabric by the measurement indicated in the directions either once or twice and ironing to make a firm crease. Sew the fold down and the hem is complete. A double-fold hem finishes a raw edge.

Darts: Darts are triangle-shaped tucks made in the fabric to create a pronounced, three-dimensional shape in the fabric piece. These are made by folding the triangle mark in half and sewing along one edge of the triangle. If the dart is big enough, cut it open and press the halves outward. If not, press it to one side.

Gathering: Ruffles or gathers are made in fabric by sewing two lines of very long straight stitches (without backstitching) within the seam allowance of your fabric piece. Tie the threads at one end of the fabric and pull on the bobbin threads at the other end. Once the piece is gathered to the desired size, knot the bobbin threads and machine sew the edge to hold the gathers in place.

Darts. Darts create a three-dimensional shape in otherwise two-dimensional fabric.

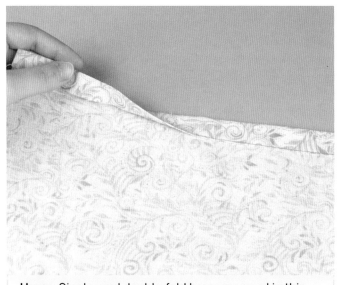

Hems. Single- and double-fold hems are used in this book for unfinished edges.

Gathers. When you pull at the bobbin threads of a seam with very long stitches, ruffles are made in the fabric.

Sewing Knit Fabrics

Once you've gotten a handle on sewing with different weights and textures of woven fabrics, why not try out knits? They can be a little unpredictable at times, and that's why it helps to have some background knowledge about fabrics so you can be ready for anything unexpected the knits might throw at you.

Varieties of knits: As mentioned in the fabrics section (page 14), there are large varieties of light- and medium-weight knits to choose from. Medium-weight knits typically stretch less than lightweight knits and are therefore easier to sew. Start with the thicker varieties before working your way down to slinkier fabrics.

Knit grain lines: It's very important to keep to your grain line when working with knits. Because knits stretch across the horizontal grain (and sometimes also the vertical grain), it's crucial that the pattern pieces line up to go along with this stretch. A tote bag that only stretches vertically will sag lower and lower over time, but if you cut your fabric for it so it stretches horizontally, you can enjoy the feel of t-shirt fabric without the stretchiness getting you down. So think one step ahead if you can and imagine where the fabric should and shouldn't stretch when you cut it.

Cutting knits: Some lightweight knits can be slinky and move in unpredictable ways while you cut them. A good way to tame these fabrics is to lay them on tissue paper (or newspaper if you don't mind washing off ink) before you cut them. As you pin your pieces and cut them, make sure you go through all the layers. Try to downgrade to your craft scissors for this if possible, as the tissue paper can dull your sewing shears.

Sewing needle for knits: There are special sewing machine needles designed for knit fabrics. They have a rounded tip that allows the needle to punch between the threads rather than right through. If your seams aren't turning out how you'd like, check to be sure that you're using a sewing needle for knits.

Stretch stitches: Because your finished garment will be stretchy, your seams should stretch along with it or the threads might break. If your machine has a stretch stitch, then you're in business! It will often use a kind of two-steps-forward, one-step-back motion that works to give the garment some stretch. If your machine doesn't have a stretch stitch, a zigzag stitch with a narrow width and medium length is a great substitute.

The problem with knits: The main issue with knits is how they tend to stretch while you sew them. No matter how little you touch the fabric, the pressure of the presser foot and the pulling of the needle seem to do something that gives you warped, wavy seams—especially at the hems. However, once you finally get things working in your favor and your seams are perfectly flat and neat, knits are joy to work with! Your seams will look much more fluid and smooth, your garments will fit you comfortably and perfectly, and you don't have to worry about finished seams! Knits don't unravel, so putting together knit projects is super quick! Here are some tips for keeping your knits from stretching out of shape while you sew:

Hands off: Even if you might not realize it, you could be pushing or pulling at your fabric while you sew. Try to consciously put less pressure on the fabric while you guide it and your seams might turn out better.

Cutting knits: Cut your knit fabrics with a layer of tissue or newspaper underneath for more stability, but be sure to use craft scissors if you can.

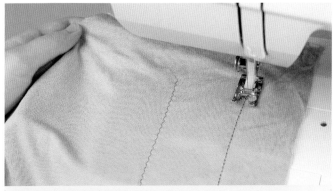

Stretch stitches: A narrow zigzag stitch or machine stretch stitch will allow your seams to stretch along with your knit fabrics.

Ease the presser foot: If your machine has an adjustable presser control for the presser foot, bring it down to the lowest pressure (but not 0). The presser foot won't push down as much on the fabric, so it won't cause it to stretch.

Easing: Easing is a technique usually used for woven fabrics to give the fabric a light, even, and almost unnoticeable distribution of gathers along an edge. In knit fabrics, this works to prevent stretched stitches and puckers. While you sew your seam, press down behind the fabric so the fabric feeding through the machine begins to build up. Your sewing will start to slow down, and when it slows to almost no motion, let the fabric go and press your finger down again.

Stabilizing: If your knits are still giving you trouble, especially if they are thin enough that the needle forces them down through the throat plate, stabilizer is a very reliable solution. Use tissue paper, newspaper, or very lightweight stabilizer beneath your fabric as you sew. When you finish, gently tear the paper away from your stitches to avoid breaking them.

Ironing: Even if your stitches seem a little wobbly after you sew, try giving them an iron to see if they smooth out. In a lot of cases they will improve quite a bit, so there's no need to worry about how your seams look right out of the machine.

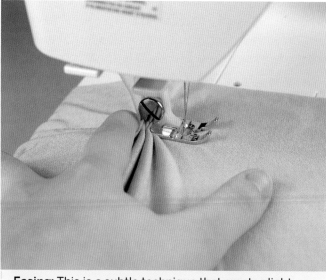

Easing: This is a subtle technique that creates light gathers in your fabric, effectively canceling out the stretching that might happen while you sew knits.

Stabilizing your stitches: As a trump card, layering tissue or newspaper beneath your fabric will stop any stretching dead in its tracks. Just be careful when tearing away the paper afterward.

Appliqué

Appliqué is one of the main embellishment techniques used in this book to decorate projects. It is the process of sewing one small shape of fabric on top of another larger piece for decorative purposes. For machine appliqué, however, there are a few different methods that can suit your skill level, resources, or desired look.

APPLIQUÉ SUPPLIES

The simplest version of appliqué can be done with fabrics that are lighter than the base fabric, such as cotton or twill. More professional-looking appliqué can be achieved by adding fusible web and stabilizer.

Fabrics: Most every kind of fabric can be appliquéd, and a good rule of thumb is to use a fabric that is lighter than the fabric you're appliquéing on. Fabrics like cotton, flannel, and felt are a good choice, but even thinner twill, home décor, and faux suede fabrics would work well. Most of these fabrics will fray if their raw edges are exposed. That could be the look you're going for, but if not, be sure to choose your appliqué method accordingly.

Fusible web: Used in this book for appliqué, fusible web is a paper-backed adhesive. When it's ironed to almost any fabric, it makes it an iron-on patch. This patch can then be adhered and sewn to your project with ease. It is nearly indispensible for small and lightweight appliqué pieces. However, it is optional for larger, thicker pieces of appliqué, which may only need some sewing pins to hold them in place. The lightweight variety of fusible web is ideal for sewn appliqué and is sold by the yard or in precut packages.

Appliqué supplies: Appliqué can easily be done using the fabric of your choice and fusible web and stabilizer for extra support.

Stabilizer: Often used in tandem with fusible web, stabilizer prevents warping and shifting of fabric during the appliqué process. It's very helpful for lightweight appliqué pieces and when using the satin stitch method, but is less necessary for more stable fabrics or when using the straight and zigzag stitch methods. Lightweight to medium-weight stabilizer suits appliqué best and can be found by the yard or in precut packages.

APPLIQUÉ TECHNIQUES

Applying one decorative fabric to another can be done in a number of different ways. You can choose which one you like depending on the difficulty or finished look you are going for. Here are some easy and surefire methods you can try:

Adhesive method:

Fusible web: Heavy-duty
Stitch: None
Fabric: Felt

This method uses only fusible web to adhere the appliqué fabric. This is a great simple method for projects that won't receive a lot of washing. After applying the fusible web to your appliqué fabric, iron it to your finished project following the manufacturer's instructions. Just like an iron-on patch, the heavy-duty adhesive will hold the fabric there indefinitely!

Floating method:

Fusible web: None
Stitch: Straight
Fabric: Felt

This is what I use to describe the appliqué method in which only a small section of the fabric is sewn down and the rest floats free for a charming three-dimensional effect. Lay your appliqué fabric onto your main fabric and sew it down with a straight stitch along the lines the pattern indicates, typically along the center of the piece.

Straight stitch method:

Fusible web: Light
Stitch: Straight
Fabric: Felt

With this method, you stitch the edges of your appliqué fabric completely to your main fabric, but you do so easily with just a straight stitch. Use fusible web to adhere your appliqué fabric to the main fabric. Sew along the edge of the appliqué fabric, about ⅛" (0.5cm) in from the edge.

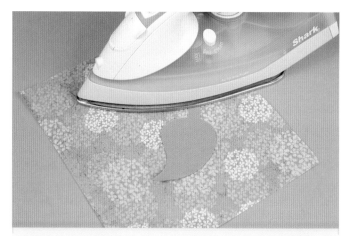

Adhesive method: With just some heavy-duty fusible web, you can iron on any felt appliqué as easily as an iron-on patch.

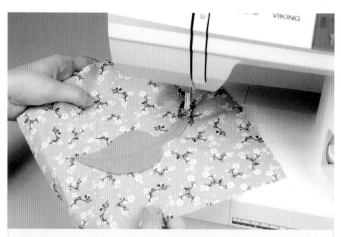

Floating method: A simple straight stitch down the middle of a felt shape is enough to hold it in place and leaves the rest free for added dimension.

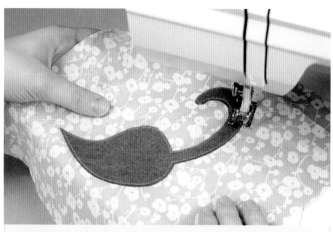

Straight stitch method: Choose a contrasting color thread for a cute shabby-chic look.

Zigzag method:

Fusible web: Light
Stitch: Zigzag
Fabric: Felt or cotton

This method takes longer than those listed on page 38, but allows you to use cotton as your appliqué fabric without fear of it unraveling. Adhere your appliqué fabric to the main fabric with fusible web. Using a zigzag stitch of short length (0.75–1.25) and medium to wide width (2–4.5), sew along the edges of the appliqué fabric, covering the raw edge of the fabric.

Satin stitch method:

Fusible web: Medium-weight
Stitch: Zigzag
Fabric: Felt or cotton

After applying the appliqué pieces, sew a medium to wide width and very short length (usually the shortest your machine can handle) zigzag stitch over the edge of the pieces. This takes more patience and coordination, but yields a very professional result. Medium-weight stabilizer is recommended, because the dense stitches can warp the main fabric.

This option completely encases the raw edges of the appliqué piece in thread, so there is no need to worry about unraveling. Complementary thread colors can also be used, and embroidery threads work especially well in this application, as the finished product has a beautiful sheen.

Zigzag method: Use a narrow width zigzag stitch for small appliqué pieces and a wider stitch for larger pieces.

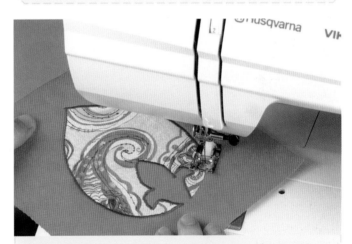

Satin stitch: This appliqué method uses a medium to wide width zigzag stitch at the shortest of lengths. The stitches are so close that no fabric from the appliqué piece peeks through and a professional-looking line of stitches is created.

Following the Projects

Now that you've refreshed yourself on the basics, it's time to dive into your first project. The projects in this book generally work from the simplest to the most time-intensive and complex, allowing you to improve your skills as you go. There will be lots of other useful sewing tips and techniques to learn along the way as well.

With each project, you'll find a tools and materials list, listing all the fabric and other supplies you'll need, as well as in what quantities. Fabrics come in varying widths and the materials list will state how many yards you'll need depending on the width. If the list doesn't specify, then either width is fine. The tools you need are also listed, including your basic sewing kit and any additional tools.

Although every project is suitable for beginners, you'll find that they are rated from one to eight stars based on the estimated time needed, the additional techniques used, and the overall complexity of the project.

⭐ If you've never picked up a needle, start with these! They usually require one to three very easy techniques and take mere minutes to make.

⭐⭐ Your beginner's jitters have worn off and you're not so anxious to cut into your fabric anymore. These projects require one to three simple techniques or take about an hour to make.

⭐⭐⭐ You're starting to understand the basic principles and are eager to see how they work together. These projects require two to four simple techniques or take a little more than an hour or so to make.

⭐⭐⭐⭐ You've had a few ah-ha! moments and new techniques sound exciting rather than scary to you. These projects may have one or two intermediate techniques or take between one and two hours to make.

⭐⭐⭐⭐⭐ Using your machine has started to become natural, and you barely have to look at your manual or cheat sheet anymore. These projects may have two or three intermediate techniques or take two hours or so to make.

⭐⭐⭐⭐⭐⭐ Using techniques now feels completely natural and you barely have to check up on how to do them anymore. These projects may have three or four intermediate techniques or take between two and three hours to make.

⭐⭐⭐⭐⭐⭐⭐ The mechanics of sewing and assembling fabric pieces now start to make sense, and you can see where your project is going as you assemble it. These projects may have one or two advanced techniques or take about an afternoon of work to make.

⭐⭐⭐⭐⭐⭐⭐⭐ You feel like you're really in the zone and you're ready to take on anything! These projects have three or four advanced techniques or take a few afternoons of work to make.

USING THE PATTERNS

Each project comes with pattern pieces either printed in the book with the project or listed as squares that you should cut. The printed patterns can be enlarged at a copy center or on your personal computer so they can be cut out with craft scissors.

The printed patterns list everything you need to know so you can work with them in the easiest way possible, including the pattern piece name, the seam allowance, the seam line, the number you should cut, and what fabric and color you should cut it from if applicable.

Each pattern also has a grain line, which indicates in what direction the pattern should be placed when it's cut from the fabric.

For square patterns, the project will list dimensions you can use to cut the pieces straight from your fabric without requiring a pattern piece. However, because it's always smarter to measure twice and cut once, I sometimes like to measure these pattern pieces from newspaper and use those on the fabric rather than cutting straight from the material.

Stars to Caffeine!

Ranking these projects with stars is very straightforward and easy to follow—perfect if you're just starting out. I must confess that I'm a bit of a foodie, though, so I often think of the level of difficulty of each project in terms of food. For example: sourness! In this case, the easiest projects might be called tangerines, and the hardest projects grapefruits. Or spiciness, where the easiest projects are green peppers and the hardest are ghost peppers! One of my favorite ways to think about project difficulty is by level of caffeine. Easier projects are perfect for working during a lazy afternoon and sipping your favorite cup of green tea, while for the harder ones, you might need to break out the espresso! If I were to translate these projects to level of caffeine, this is what they would look like:

White Tea	Green Tea	Black Tea	Cappuccino	Latte	Cuppa' Joe	French Roast	Espresso

If you were to choose a way to represent a project's difficulty level, how would you do it?

PREPARING YOUR FABRIC

When you have your fabrics ready for your project, you should first be sure to prewash them if they're brand new. Fabric bolts at the store list the washing instructions, though basic beginner fabrics rarely require special washing processes. Prewashing eliminates the light starch that tends to be applied to retail fabrics, and it also gets any shrinkage out of the way.

If your fabric is wrinkle-prone, be sure to iron it smooth before cutting from it. The most typical way to cut pattern pieces is to fold the fabric in half so the selvedge edges meet. The selvedge edges are the machine-finished edges of your fabric; you'll notice that they're a lot stiffer than the rest of the fabric. Check to see if your fabric has a direction to it. If the prints or designs all point in one direction, you'll want your pattern pieces aligned so the pattern matches. It's a persnickety thing, so it's only really important with big

graphics. You'd hate to have your new purse covered with upside-down flowers! To assist with this, the grain lines on each pattern piece indicate the direction the design should point in. For the best results, make sure the grain line is parallel to the selvedge edge of your fabric.

Next, you'll want to pin your pattern pieces to your fabric exactly the same way as pinning fabric together. Weave the pins in then out of the layers of fabric and paper. Pin down all your pattern pieces at once, trying to leave as little space between them as possible to get the most out of your fabric. Because you're cutting your fabric on a folded sheet, notice that you'll get two pieces at once. This is not only a time saver, but it's typical practice in sewing, as most projects are designed to be symmetrical. Your pattern will indicate how many pieces you need to cut. It's usually two, but if not, unfold your fabric before cutting.

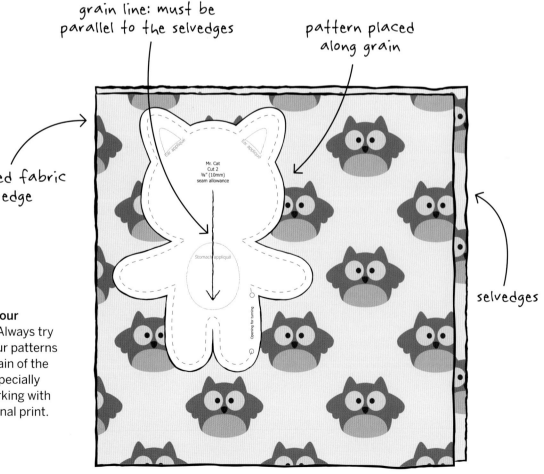

grain line: must be parallel to the selvedges

pattern placed along grain

folded fabric edge

Mr. Cat
Cut 2
⅜" (10mm)
seam allowance

selvedges

Placing your pattern: Always try to cut your patterns on the grain of the fabric, especially when working with a directional print.

CUTTING YOUR PATTERN PIECES

Once you have all your pattern pieces pinned, it's time to cut them out. Cut as closely as possible to the outside edge of your patterns. If your scissors are sharp, you shouldn't have any issue getting clean and smooth cuts.

When all your pieces are cut from the fabric, begin to remove your patterns. Using your fabric marker, transfer any markings from the patterns to the fabric. Check the project page for any additional markings that need to be made. Another helpful trick is to label your pattern pieces. If you have adhesive labels on hand, those are perfect, but masking tape works well in a pinch. Label the right side of the fabric, and write the name of the pattern piece so you'll know when to use it. Now you'll always know what side is the right side and make sure to match it up!

All of this prep work may seem tedious, but you can take it from me that it's well worth the extra time and saves headaches and confusion in the long run. Often this start-up work takes up about half the time I spend on a project (don't worry, this time is reflected in the project time estimates!), so once you finish you can feel like you're nearly halfway there!

Label & mark your pieces: Transfer all the markings and notes from the pattern to your fabric and it will be a huge help as you embark on your project.

sew me!
Sew and Go Projects

Now that you've given yourself a refresher course on the techniques you'll need to use, you are ready to get sewing! Use the projects in this chapter to jazz up your wardrobe, add a special touch to your favorite book or journal, or infuse your electronic devices with your personal style. Use each project as an opportunity to express yourself, whether it's through your fabric selection or the appliqué design you choose to use. If you don't love it, don't sew it.

46 Simple Cell Phone Case

50 Book Cover

54 Book Bandolier

58 Tablet Sleeve

67 Roll-Up Pencil Case

73 Drawstring Ditty Bag

78 Reversible Tote Bag

83 Mini Messenger Bag

88 Polished Ruffled Purse

Simple Cell Phone Case

★☆☆☆☆☆☆☆

⏱ **ESTIMATED TIME:**
20–40 minutes

🧵 **TECHNIQUES:**
Appliqué, Lining

✓ **MAKES:**
One 2¼" x 6" (5.5 x 15cm) case,
sized to fit an iPhone 6

This perfectly sized case will keep your phone snug and safe while you stash it away in your pocket, bag, or purse. Plus, you can individualize it just to your taste with an adorable robot, starburst, or crown appliqué design.

Materials

- ☐ ¼ yd. (25cm) or 10" x 10" (25.5 x 25.5cm) scrap of light- to medium-weight woven fabric for outside case
- ☐ ¼ yd. (25cm) or 10" x 10" (25.5 x 25.5cm) scrap of lightweight woven fabric for lining
- ☐ Fat quarter or 6" x 6" (15 x 15cm) scrap of appliqué fabric (optional)
- ☐ 6" x 6" (15 x 15cm) square of fusible web (optional)

Tools

- ☐ Basic sewing kit (see page 25)
- ☐ Chopstick or similar turning tool

Your collection of fabric pieces for this project should look something like this:

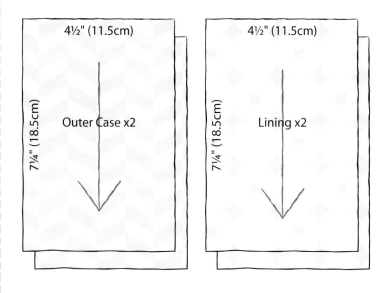

THE PREP WORK:

Cut your fabric pieces using the following chart. Cut any additional appliqué pieces from the patterns on page 49. The measurements listed below are for an iPhone 6. For other iPhone sizes, use the following measurements: iPhone 5C or 5S (4¼" x 6¾" [11 x 17cm]), iPhone 6 Plus (5" x 8" [12.5 x 20.5cm]).

Simple Cell Phone Case Pieces

Piece Name	Material to Cut	Size to Cut	Number to Cut	Seam Allowance
Outer Case	Light- to medium-weight woven	4½" x 7¼" (11.5 x 18.5cm)	2	⅝" (1.5cm)
Lining	Lightweight woven	4½" x 7¼" (11.5 x 18.5cm)	2	⅝" (1.5cm)

Simple Cell Phone Case (continued)

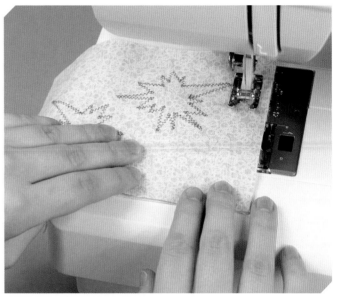

1 **Appliqué your design (optional).** See the Getting Started chapter (page 37) to choose a method for applying your decorative fabric to the outer case. Sew your appliqué in the center of one or both of the outer case pieces, or at least 1" (2.5cm) in from the edge of the fabric.

2 **Sew the top edges.** Align one outer case piece with one lining piece along the top edge with right sides facing. Sew along the top edge only. Repeat with the remaining outer case and lining pieces. Iron the seams open.

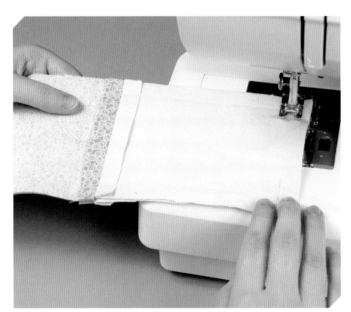

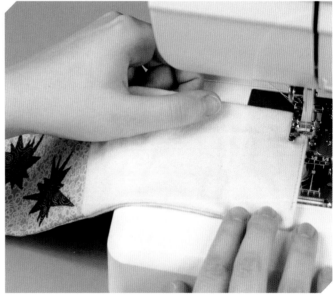

3 **Sew the case.** Mark a 2" (5cm) line on the wrong side of each lining piece, centering it along the bottom edge. This marks your opening for turning. Match up the raw edges of the outer case pieces and the lining pieces with right sides together, and pin them in place. Sew entirely around the perimeter, skipping over the line marked on the lining pieces. Clip the seam allowances at the corners, turn the case right side out, and press the seams.

4 **Sew the opening closed.** Fold in the seam allowances around the opening in the lining, and machine sew along the opening, close to the edge of the folds, to close it. Tuck the lining into the outer case and iron the top edge.

Simple Cell Phone Case Patterns

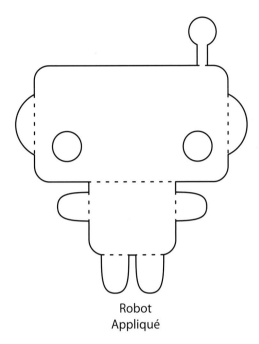

Robot
Appliqué

Crown
Appliqué

Starburst
Appliqué

Patterns shown at actual size.

Book Cover

★ ★ ☆ ☆ ☆ ☆ ☆ ☆

🕐 **ESTIMATED TIME:**
30–60 minutes

TECHNIQUES:
Appliqué, Interfacing,
Ladder Stitch

✓ **MAKES:**
One cover sized to fit your book

Materials

☐ Light- to medium-weight woven fabric in length B (rounded up to the nearest ¼ yd. [25cm] for insurance)

☐ Lightweight fusible interfacing in length B x 2 (rounded up to the nearest ¼ yd. [25cm] for insurance)

☐ Fat quarter or 10" x 10" (25.5 x 25.5cm) scrap of appliqué fabric (optional)

☐ 10" x 10" (25.5 x 25.5cm) square of fusible web (optional)

Tools

☐ Basic sewing kit (see page 25)

☐ Chopstick or similar turning tool

If you have a favorite book, whether it is a beloved photo album or a worn-down classic, this book cover will give that cherished item the unique look and protection it deserves. You make it exactly to your book's measurements, so it is sure to fit perfectly, and the added moon, rabbit, and tree appliqué make it extra special. Or create an appliqué pattern that hints at what's inside!

MEASUREMENTS

Work out these equations to find out what size pieces to cut. Feel free to round up to the nearest ¼" (0.5cm) for each final measurement to make things easier.

Full cover width + 1½" (4cm) = _____ A (Cover width)

Book length + 1½" (4cm) = _____ B (Cover length)

Front cover width = _____ C

Follow these steps to get your last measurement:

Take C and multiply it by 0.6 = _____

Take this new number and add 1" (2.5cm) = _____

Take this new number and multiply it by 2 = _____ D (Pocket width)

Measure the length and width of your book to determine the dimensions of your cover.

Front cover width

Book length

Full cover width

Book Cover *(continued)*

Your collection of fabric pieces for this project should look something like this:

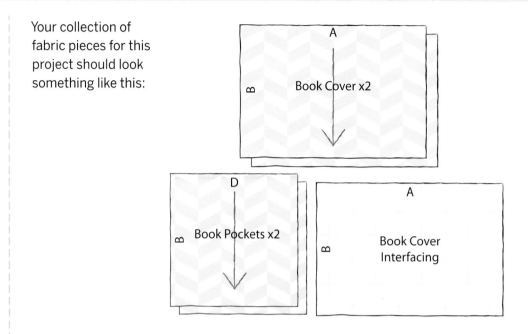

THE PREP WORK:

Cut your fabric pieces using the following chart. Cut any additional appliqué pieces from the patterns on page 53.

Book Cover Pieces

Piece Name	Material to Cut	Size to Cut	Number to Cut	Seam Allowance
Book Cover	Light- to medium-weight woven	A x B	2	⅝" (1.5cm)
Book Cover Interfacing	Lightweight interfacing	A x B	1	⅝" (1.5cm)
Book Pockets	Light- to medium-weight woven	D x B	2	⅝" (1.5cm)

1 **Appliqué your design (optional).** See the Getting Started chapter (page 37) to choose a method for applying your decorative fabric to the book cover. Sew your appliqué on the right side of the book cover fabric, at least 1" (2.5cm) in from the edge. If you want your appliqué to appear on the front of the book cover, stitch it to the right side of the fabric. For the back, stitch it to the left side.

2 **Apply the interfacing.** Place the interfacing over the book cover fabric with the appliqué. Following the manufacturer's directions, fuse it completely to the wrong side of the fabric.

Book Cover (continued)

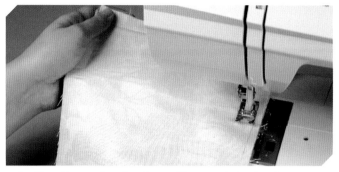

3 **Baste the pockets.** Fold each pocket in half widthwise with wrong sides together. Line up the raw edges of each pocket with the short ends of the book cover fabric with the appliqué attached. Place the pockets on the right side of the fabric. Baste the pockets along the three raw edges within the seam allowances to hold them in place for Step 4.

4 **Sew the perimeter.** Layer the remaining book cover piece on top of the front piece with right sides together. Mark a 5" (12.5cm) line on the wrong side of the book cover fabric, centering it along the bottom edge between the pockets. This marks your opening for turning. Sew around the perimeter of the book cover, skipping over this line.

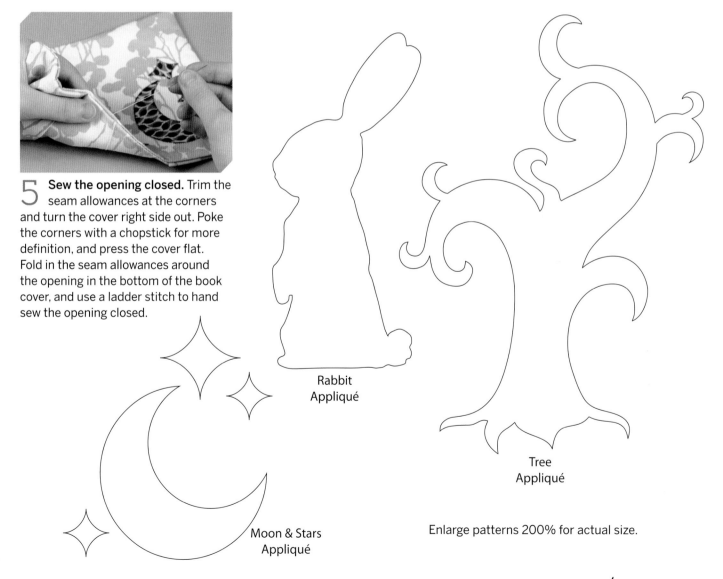

5 **Sew the opening closed.** Trim the seam allowances at the corners and turn the cover right side out. Poke the corners with a chopstick for more definition, and press the cover flat. Fold in the seam allowances around the opening in the bottom of the book cover, and use a ladder stitch to hand sew the opening closed.

Rabbit Appliqué

Tree Appliqué

Moon & Stars Appliqué

Enlarge patterns 200% for actual size.

Book Bandolier

★ ★ ☆ ☆ ☆ ☆ ☆ ☆

ESTIMATED TIME:
30–60 minutes

TECHNIQUES:
Hook-and-Loop Tape

MAKES:
One 30" (76cm) strap with
4 pencil pockets

If you, or someone you know, are an avid drawer, this is the perfect project! This handy strap makes taking your favorite pens and pencils with you a breeze. Wrap it around a sketchbook, binder, or notepad so you always have your pencils on hand.

Materials

☐ ⅓ yd. (33cm) of lightweight woven fabric

☐ 20" (51cm) of ¾" (2cm)-wide hook-and-loop tape

Tools

☐ Basic sewing kit (see page 25)

☐ Chopstick or similar turning tool

Your collection of fabric pieces for this project should look something like this:

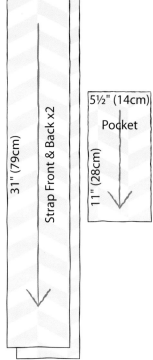

THE PREP WORK:

Cut your fabric pieces using the following chart.

Book Bandolier Pieces

Piece Name	Material to Cut	Size to Cut	Number to Cut	Seam Allowance
Strap Front & Back	Lightweight woven	5½" x 31" (14 x 79cm)	2	⅝" (1.5cm)
Pocket	Lightweight woven	5½" x 11" (14 x 28cm)	1	⅝" (1.5cm)

Book Bandolier *(continued)*

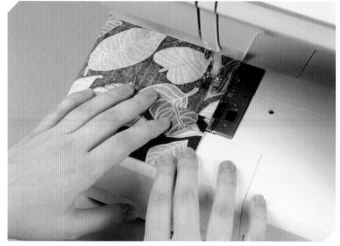

1 **Prepare the pocket.** Mark a horizontal line across the right side of the front strap piece, 12½" (31.5cm) from one of the short ends. This marks the placement of the pocket. Fold the pocket piece in half widthwise with right sides together, and sew along the open edge where the two fabric ends come together. Turn the pocket right side out and press.

2 **Apply the pocket.** Line up the bottom of the pocket with the line drawn on the front strap piece. Place the folded edge of the pocket so it points toward the top of the strap. Sew close to the bottom edge of the pocket; this is known as edge stitching. Baste the pocket to the strap by sewing along the sides, within the seam allowances.

3 **Sew the strap.** Layer the strap back over the strap front (with attached pocket) with right sides facing. Draw a 5" (12.5cm) line along one side of the strap between the pocket and bottom edge. This marks your opening for turning. Sew around the entire strap, skipping over the marked line. Trim the seam allowances, turn the strap right side out, poke the corners with a chopstick for definition, and iron the strap flat.

4 **Edge stitch the strap.** Fold in the seam allowances around the opening in the strap's side, and iron them flat. Sew around the entire perimeter of the strap, stitching close to the outside edge, about ⅛" (0.5cm) from the seam. This will sew the opening closed.

Book Bandolier *(continued)*

5 **Apply the hook-and-loop tape.** Cut five 3½" (9cm) pieces of hook-and-loop tape from the loop side and three 6½" (16.5cm) pieces of hook-and-loop tape from the hook side. Sew the 3½" (9cm) pieces to the strap front, parallel to the short bottom edge. Sew one piece along the bottom edge, and then sew the others parallel to it, spacing them about ¾" (2cm) apart. Sew the 6½" (16.5cm) pieces on the back of the strap at the opposite end. Position the 6½" pieces so their long edges are parallel with the long edges of the strap. Sew one piece along the upper right side, and then sew the others parallel to it, spacing them about ¾" (2cm) apart. This means the hook-and-loop pieces will be perpendicular to one another when the ends of the strap are attached. See the illustration at the right for help with this step.

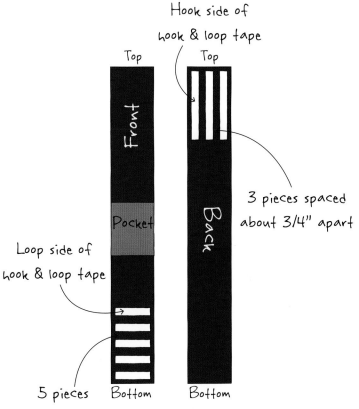

6 **Complete the pocket.** Mark the separations for the pocket by drawing vertical lines on the pocket front at 1", 2", and 3" (2.5, 5, and 7.5cm) in from one of the stitch lines. Sew along these lines so the pocket has four slots for your pens and pencils.

Tablet Sleeve

★★★☆☆☆☆

ESTIMATED TIME:
45–90 minutes

TECHNIQUES:
Interfacing, Buttons
& Buttonholes

MAKES:
One sleeve sized to match your
tablet/e-book reader

Tablets and e-book readers are so handy, it's hard not to take them everywhere. Make them safer for travel with this charming padded tablet sleeve. It's sized to match your tablet perfectly so it fits snugly and safely without a chance of scratches. Also customize it to make it your own with the additional koi, bamboo, or retro game sprite appliqué!

Materials

- ☐ ½ yd. (50cm) of lightweight woven fabric for outside
- ☐ ½ yd. (50cm) of lightweight woven fabric for lining
- ☐ ⅓ yd. (33cm) of lightweight fusible interfacing
- ☐ ⅓ yd. (33cm) of quilt batting or fleece for padding
- ☐ One button, about ½" to 1¼" (1.5 to 3cm) in diameter
- ☐ Fat quarter or 10" x 10" (25.5 x 25.5cm) scrap of appliqué fabric (optional)
- ☐ 10" x 10" (25.5 x 25.5cm) square of fusible web (optional)

Tools

- ☐ Basic sewing kit (see page 25)
- ☐ Chopstick or similar turning tool

MEASUREMENTS

Work out these equations to find out what size pieces to cut. Feel free to round up to the nearest ¼" (0.5cm) for each final measurement to make things easier.

Tablet width + 3" (7.5cm) = _____ A (Cover width)

Tablet length + 3" (7.5cm) = _____ B (Cover length)

Tablet length × 0.85 + 2" (5cm) = _____ C (Pocket length)

Tablet length × 1.5 + 3" (7.5cm) = _____ D (Flap length)

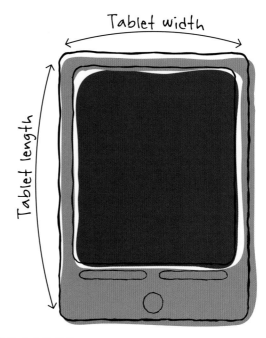

Tablet width

Tablet length

Tablet Sleeve (continued)

Your collection of fabric pieces for this project should look something like this:

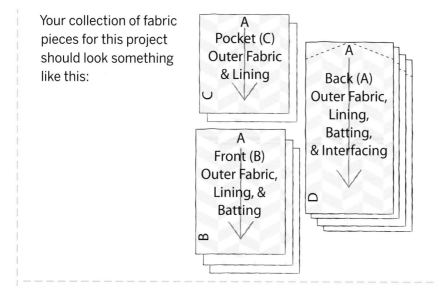

THE PREP WORK:

Cut your fabric pieces using the following chart. Cut any additional appliqué pieces from the patterns on page 66.

Tablet Sleeve Pieces

Piece Name	Material to Cut	Size to Cut	Number to Cut	Seam Allowance
Back (A) Outer Fabric	Lightweight woven	A x D	1	⅝" (1.5cm)
Back (A) Lining	Lightweight woven	A x D	1	⅝" (1.5cm)
Back (A) Batting	Batting	A x D	1	⅝" (1.5cm)
Back (A) Interfacing	Lightweight interfacing	A x D	1	⅝" (1.5cm)
Front (B) Outer Fabric	Lightweight woven	A x B	1	⅝" (1.5cm)
Front (B) Lining	Lightweight woven	A x B	1	⅝" (1.5cm)
Front (B) Batting	Batting	A x B	1	⅝" (1.5cm)
Pocket (C) Outer Fabric	Lightweight woven	A x C	1	⅝" (1.5cm)
Pocket (C) Lining	Lightweight woven	A x C	1	⅝" (1.5cm)

1 **Apply the interfacing.** Place the interfacing for the back over the back fabric (A). Following the manufacturer's directions, fuse the interfacing completely to the wrong side of the fabric.

2 **Cut the flap shape.** Trim the top edge of the back (A) to a point. To do this, mark the center point of the top edge of the back. Then, multiply the length of your tablet by 0.2. Starting at the top left corner, measure this amount down from the top edge and make a mark. Draw a line from this point to the center point of the top edge, and trim the fabric along this line. Repeat for the opposite side. This should create a pointed shape.

Tablet Sleeve *(continued)*

3 **Appliqué your design (optional).** See the Getting Started chapter (page 37) to choose a method for applying your decorative fabric to the outer fabric of the back (A). Sew your appliqué at least 1" (2.5cm) in from the sides or bottom of the back so your image won't be cut off.

4 **Sew the front and pocket.** Layer the outer fabric and lining pieces for the front (B) together with right sides facing and the lining piece on top. Layer the batting piece underneath them, and sew all three layers together along the top edge. Flip the lining piece over to the other side of the batting so the lining is on one side of the batting and the outer fabric is on the other. Press the seam, and then edge stitch close to the seam for a finished look. Repeat this with the pocket pieces (C), but without the batting.

5 **Layer the pieces.** Layer the pieces as follows: back batting, back lining (A), front (B), pocket (C), and then back outer fabric (A). All pieces should be right side up, except for the back outer fabric, which faces down. Mark a 5" (12.5cm) line on the wrong side of the back outer fabric, centering it along the bottom edge. This marks your opening for turning.

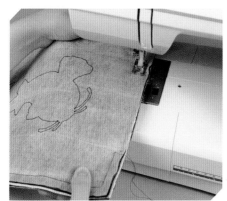

6 **Sew the layers.** Sew around the entire perimeter of the sleeve, skipping over the marked line. Trim the seam allowances, turn the sleeve right side out, poke the corners with a chopstick, and press the seams.

7 **Edge stitch the sleeve.** Fold in the seam allowances around the opening in the bottom edge and iron them flat. Edge stitch around the perimeter of the sleeve, about ⅛" (0.5cm) from the outer seam. This will close the opening.

8 **Add the button and buttonhole.** Mark a buttonhole centered on the flap point about ½" (1.5cm) up from the point. Follow the buttonhole instructions on page 62 to make a buttonhole here. Close the flap and use the buttonhole to mark the placement for your button on the outside of the sleeve. Then, sew the button in place.

Buttons and Buttonholes

Buttons and buttonholes are a kind of closure that can be used in accessories or clothing. They are perfect if you want to show off a decorative button, but I think their best attribute is that they are less likely to scratch or poke you when you least expect it like zippers, hook-and-loop tape, or snaps might do.

Sewing a buttonhole: A buttonhole is essentially a square of tight zigzag stitches with a hole cut in the center for the button to slip through. The zigzag stitches prevent the cut edges from unraveling. If you have a sewing machine with a buttonhole function, a precise square is very easy to make, but here are some pointers to make sure you understand how your machine does it.

1 **Apply interfacing.** Buttonholes should be stabilized with interfacing so the dense stitches don't warp the fabric. Apply the selected interfacing to the wrong side of your fabric before sewing the buttonholes.

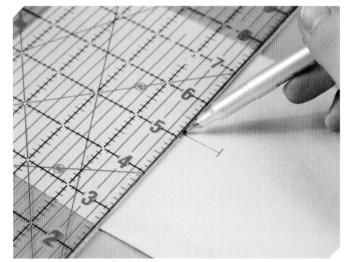

2 **Mark your buttonholes.** Accurately mark your pattern for where your buttonhole should go. Your lines should be equal to the diameter of your button plus ⅛" (0.5cm) for extra moving room. If your button is ball-shaped or particularly tall, add the height of the button as well. Mark two ¼" (0.5cm) perpendicular lines at the end of the buttonhole guide; this will give you extra guidance for making the buttonhole a square.

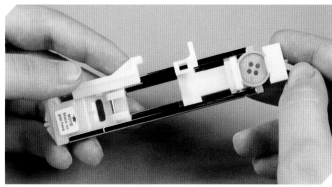

3 **For a one-step buttonhole machine: Prepare the button foot.** If your machine offers a one-step buttonhole function, it won't work properly unless you use the available buttonhole foot to measure your button. If yours is lost, you can usually order a replacement online.

4 **For a one-step buttonhole machine: Sew the buttonhole.** Install your buttonhole presser foot with the button loaded into the back. Check your manufacturer's instructions, as you might have to engage a buttonhole guide for this stitch. When you choose the buttonhole stitch from your machine, it should create the entire buttonhole when you press down the foot pedal until it finishes.

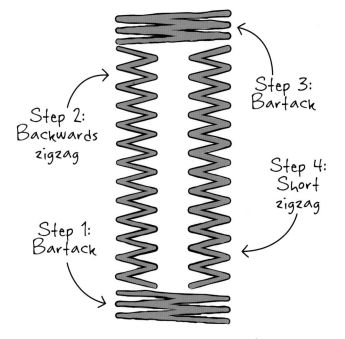

Step 3: Bartack

Step 2: Backwards zigzag

Step 4: Short zigzag

Step 1: Bartack

Four-step buttonhole: A four-step buttonhole machine will usually follow these steps to create the buttonhole.

5 **For a four-step buttonhole machine: Start the buttonhole.** Set your stitch length to very short, usually 0.5. Line up your presser foot so the needle will begin sewing to the bottom left of your center line. Select step 1, which will sew the bottom side.

6 **For a four-step buttonhole machine: Complete the buttonhole.** Select step 2, which will sew the left side of the buttonhole going backward. Step 3 will sew the top of your buttonhole. Finally, step 4 forms the right side and completes the buttonhole.

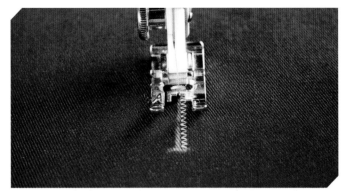

7 **For a freehand buttonhole: Sew the top side.** If for some reason you have a much older machine without a buttonhole stitch, you can still make one from scratch! It takes more precision but isn't impossible. First, set your machine to a zigzag stitch at 0.5 length and very wide (around 4–5). Sew a short bar of stitches, called a bartack, about ⅛" (0.3cm) along your top guideline.

8 **For a freehand buttonhole: Sew the right side.** Adjust your stitch width to very narrow, around 1–2, and reposition your needle so the right edge of the zigzag aligns with the right edge of your top edge. Sew all the way down to the bottom guideline.

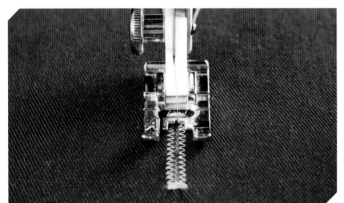

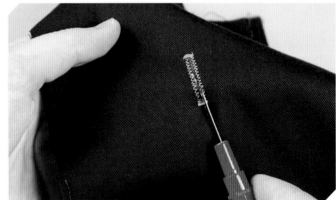

9 **For a freehand buttonhole: Complete the buttonhole.** Move your needle back to the top so the left edges match up and sew the left side. Repeat Step 7 to sew the bottom edge.

10 **For all buttonholes: Cut the center.** Using a seam ripper or very tiny and sharp scissors, cut the center of your buttonhole without clipping any of your stitches.

Sewing a button: Even non-sewers should know this technique—you can save dozens of shirts just by knowing how to reattach a lost button!

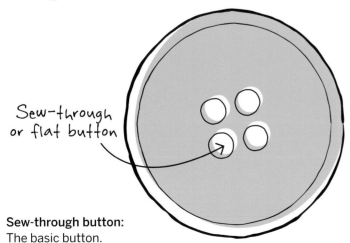

Sew-through or flat button

Sew-through button: The basic button.

Shank button

Shank button: This rounded button already has a shank, so you can skip Step 5 on the next page.

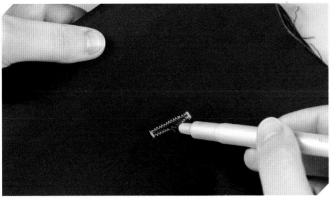

1 **Mark your placement.** Lay your finished buttonhole over the fabric where you expect the button to lie so the project looks right. Mark a dot in the center of the buttonhole to get accurate placement.

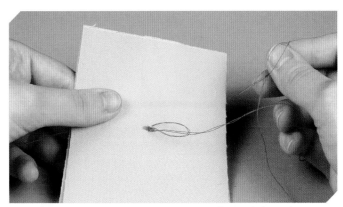

2 **Create a knot.** Prepare your needle and thread as if you were going to hand sew, creating a knot in the fabric; see the Hand Sewing feature (page 31) for more help with this. Make the knot with your thread on the place you marked.

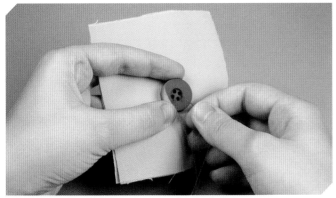

3 **Place the button.** Thread the needle through one hole in the button and hold the button in place on the fabric. Bring the needle down through the opposite buttonhole and the fabric.

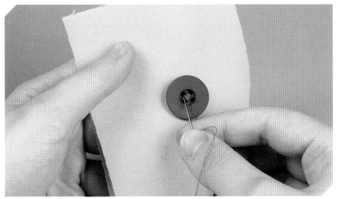

4 **Sew the button.** Continue bringing the thread up through the original buttonhole and back down into the opposite hole until the attachment feels secure (about five times). Repeat with any remaining buttonholes.

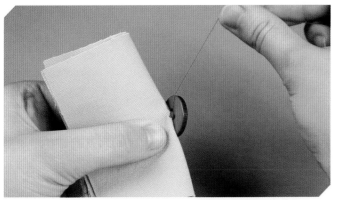

5 **Make the shank.** Bring the thread up through the fabric, but not the button. Instead, tilt the button and bring the needle out from underneath it. Wrap the thread around the stitches you've made about five times to create a shank. This creates some space between the fabric and the button. Create a knot in your fabric and clip the threads off to finish, just as in hand sewing (see page 31).

6 **For a shank button: Sew the button.** Work through Step 2 above the same as with a flat button. Instead of sewing through several buttonholes, however, continually sew through the shank in the button, and then through the fabric until the button is secure. Step 5 can be skipped because a shank is built into the button.

Tablet Sleeve Patterns

8-bit Alien
Appliqué

Koi Fish
Appliqué

Bamboo
Appliqué

Patterns shown at actual size.

Roll-Up Pencil Case

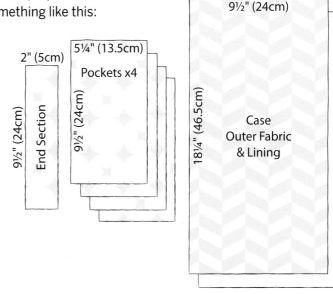

★ ★ ★ ★ ★ ☆ ☆ ☆

ESTIMATED TIME:
45–90 minutes

TECHNIQUES:
Interfacing, Appliqué, Zippers

MAKES:
One 8" x 17" (20.5 x 43cm) flat case with 4 zippered pockets

This handy case is perfect for storing little things like pencils, cosmetics, and jewelry. But it's extra handy because it rolls up and ties with attached ribbons, making it perfect for traveling. With all the pockets, all of your little trinkets will never get mixed up again! When unrolled, the large back side makes it perfect for loads of appliqué; try out the repeating star design or full dragon pattern!

Materials

- ☐ ⅓ yd. (33cm) of medium-weight fabric for outside
- ☐ ⅓ yd. (33cm) of lightweight fabric for lining
- ☐ Four 12" (30.5cm)-long zippers
- ☐ 1 yd. (100cm) of ⅝" (1.5cm)-wide ribbon
- ☐ Fat quarter or 10" x 10" (25.5 x 25.5cm) scrap of appliqué fabric (optional)
- ☐ 10" x 10" (25.5 x 25.5cm) square of fusible web (optional)

Tools

- ☐ Basic sewing kit (see page 25)
- ☐ Chopstick or similar turning tool

Your collection of fabric pieces for this project should look something like this:

THE PREP WORK:

Cut your fabric pieces using the following chart. Cut any additional appliqué pieces from the patterns on page 72.

Roll-Up Pencil Case

Piece Name	Material to Cut	Size to Cut	Number to Cut	Seam Allowance
Case Outer Fabric	Medium-weight woven	18¼" x 9½" (46.5 x 24cm)	1	⅝" (1.5cm)
Case Lining	Lightweight woven	18¼" x 9½" (46.5 x 24cm)	1	⅝" (1.5cm)
Pockets	Lightweight woven	5¼" x 9½" (13.5 x 24cm)	4	⅝" (1.5cm)
End Section	Lightweight woven	2" x 9½" (5 x 24cm)	1	⅝" (1.5cm)

Roll-Up Pencil Case (continued)

1 **Appliqué your design (optional).** See the Getting Started chapter (page 37) to choose a method for applying your decorative fabric to the outer fabric for the case. Sew your appliqué at least 1" (2.5cm) in from the edges of the fabric.

2 **Install the zippers.** Sew the four pocket pieces into a chain by stitching them together along the long edges with right sides facing. Then, sew the end section onto one end of the chain in the same manner. Finally, sew zippers into the seams, following the instructions on page 70.

3 **Create the pockets.** Place your lining piece right side up. Layer the zippered pocket piece on top, right side up, aligning the edges. Sew ¼" (0.5cm) away from the side of each zipper that is closest to the end section to create the pockets. It's important to stitch along only one side of each zipper, or you will stitch the pockets closed.

4 **Layer the pieces.** Cut your ribbon length in half. Center the end of one ribbon piece on top of the end section of the pocket piece, right side up. Lay the second ribbon piece directly on top of the first, right side down. Then, place the outer case fabric directly on top of the pocket piece, right side down. The ribbon should be sandwiched between the outer and inner case pieces with right sides together. Mark a 5" (12.5cm) line on the end opposite the ribbon, centering it along the edge of the case. This marks your opening for turning.

5 **Sew the case.** Make sure all the zipper pulls are moved toward the center of the case and pin the layers in place. Sew entirely around the perimeter of the case, going slowly when sewing over a zipper and skipping over the line marked for turning. Trim the seam allowances, turn the case right side out, poke the corners with a chopstick, and press the seams.

6 **Edge stitch the case.** Fold in the seam allowances around the opening and press them flat. Edge stitch close to the outside of the case, about ⅛" (0.5cm) from the seam. This should sew the opening closed.

Zippers

Many sewers, beginners, and frequent hobbyists alike, are deathly afraid of zippers. But I want you to know that you need not fear zippers any longer! With this foolproof method, you can be sure to master zippers and unlock a whole world of possibilities.

Varieties of zippers: Zippers can range from lightweight to heavyweight varieties. Thin coil is the lightweight option, perfect for small projects or light garments like skirts and dresses. Molded plastic is a middle-weight option, suited to jackets and heavy bags. Metal is a heavyweight option, often seen in jeans and heavy jackets. You'll see separating zippers, which are for jackets or other projects that need the zipper to separate, and also invisible zippers, which are designed for formal dresses.

Thin coil zippers are the easiest to work with and are used for the projects in this book. For the best results, stick with them, as other zippers require more practice or different techniques. Be sure to get a zipper that's the required length mentioned in the materials list, or longer. You can always shorten a zipper, but you can't lengthen one. This method of applying zippers is called the centered zipper method.

Zipper feet: Zipper feet are a special attachment that may or may not have come with your sewing machine. They replace the regular presser foot with something that looks a bit like a half foot. When you butt the zipper foot against the edge of your zipper, it allows you to sew as close as possible to the zipper without touching the teeth. Zipper feet aren't required to install the zippers here, but they do help.

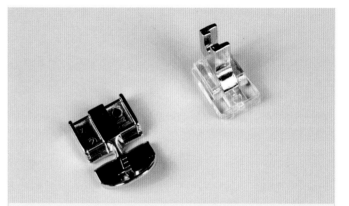

Zipper feet: If your machine came with a zipper foot, it might look something like this—sort of a half-sized foot that lets you get very close to the zipper teeth.

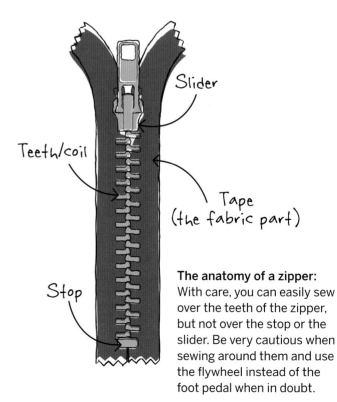

Varieties of zippers: You'll find coil, plastic, and metal varieties in the store, but coil zippers are by far the easiest to work with.

Slider

Teeth/coil

Tape (the fabric part)

Stop

The anatomy of a zipper: With care, you can easily sew over the teeth of the zipper, but not over the stop or the slider. Be very cautious when sewing around them and use the flywheel instead of the foot pedal when in doubt.

1 **Apply interfacing.** If you're working with a flimsy or even slightly stretchy fabric, fuse strips of 1" (2.5cm)-wide interfacing along the edges of your fabric pieces on the wrong side. This will keep your fabric from warping while you apply the zipper.

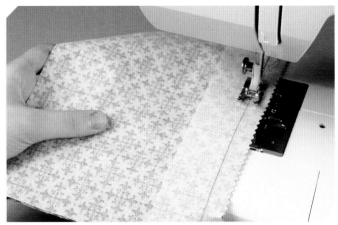

2 **Sew a straight seam.** If your project will not have a lining, be sure to finish the edges of your fabric before sewing this seam. Using a basting stitch, sew the two fabric pieces together with right sides facing, using a regular seam allowance. Press the seam fully open.

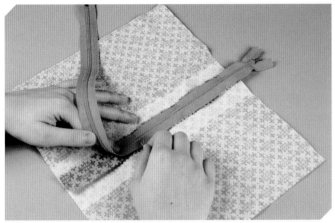

3 **Place the zipper.** Place your zipper face down on the wrong side of the seam you've created. With the projects in this book, it's fine if the beginning and end of the zipper run off the edges of the fabric. You can hold the zipper in place with pins, but scotch tape, a glue stick, or fusible web tape also work perfectly. No matter what, make sure the zipper teeth run perfectly straight down the center of the seam.

4 **Sew the zipper.** Switch to your zipper foot (if you have one) and, using a regular-length stitch, sew along one side, close to the edge of the zipper teeth. If you are making a project that has the zipper stop halfway down the fabric, you'll want to pivot your fabric and use the flywheel to slowly stitch over the zipper at the bottom end. Don't do this quickly or you could break your needle. Sew the other side of the zipper as you did the first.

5 **Remove the stitches.** Using your seam ripper, go back to the right side of your fabric and remove the stitches from the center seam. This should go smoothly because of the long stitch length. When you are finished, your zipper installation is complete, and the zipper is almost completely hidden within the seam!

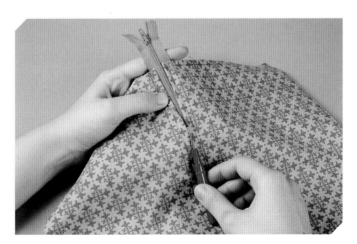

Roll-Up Pencil Case Patterns

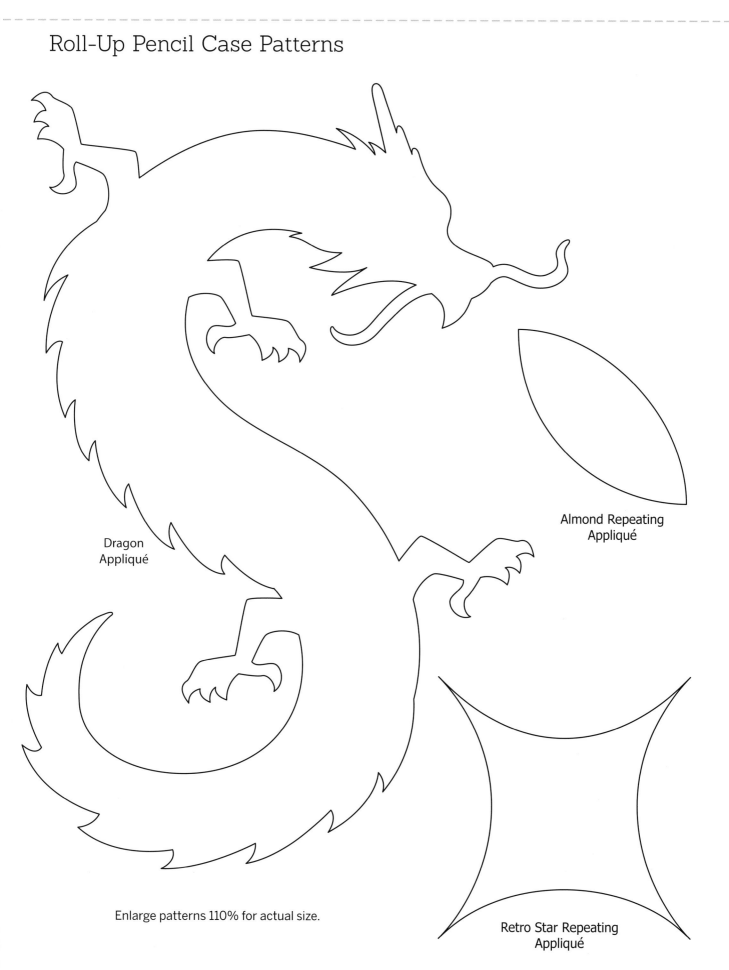

Dragon
Appliqué

Almond Repeating
Appliqué

Enlarge patterns 110% for actual size.

Retro Star Repeating
Appliqué

Drawstring Ditty Bag

★★☆☆☆☆☆☆

⏱	**ESTIMATED TIME:**	45–90 minutes
⟳	**TECHNIQUES:**	Appliqué, Lining, Drawstrings
✓	**MAKES:**	One 6½" x 7½" (16.5 x 19cm) bag

This little ditty bag is perfect for keeping anything you need to stow away. Use it to store bits like craft supplies, hold snacks or jewelry, or even use it as an elegant gift bag for someone special! The additional heart, dragonfly, and bird appliqué designs will ensure the finished product is truly you.

Materials

- ☐ ¼ yd. (25cm) of light- to medium-weight woven fabric for outer bag
- ☐ ¼ yd. (25cm) of lightweight woven fabric for lining and drawstrings
- ☐ Fat quarter or 6" x 6" (15 x 15cm) scrap of appliqué fabric (optional)
- ☐ 6" x 6" (15 x 15cm) square of fusible web (optional)

Tools

- ☐ Basic sewing kit (see page 25)
- ☐ Safety pin
- ☐ Chopstick or similar turning tool

Your collection of fabric pieces for this project should look something like this:

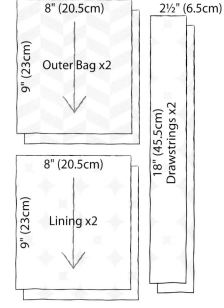

THE PREP WORK:

Cut your fabric pieces using the following chart. Cut any additional appliqué pieces from the patterns on page 77.

Drawstring Ditty Bag Pieces

Piece Name	Material to Cut	Size to Cut	Number to Cut	Seam Allowance
Outer Bag	Light- to medium-weight woven	8" x 9" (20.5 x 23cm)	2	⅝" (1.5cm)
Lining	Lightweight woven	8" x 9" (20.5 x 23cm)	2	⅝" (1.5cm)
Drawstrings	Lightweight woven	2½" x 18" (6.5 x 45.5cm)	2	⅝" (1.5cm)

Drawstring Ditty Bag (continued)

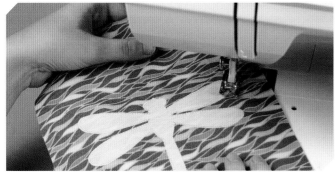

1 **Appliqué your design (optional).** See the Getting Started chapter (page 37) to choose a method for applying your decorative fabric to the outer bag. Sew your appliqué in the center of the outer bag front piece, or at least 1" (2.5cm) in from the edge of the fabric.

2 **Mark the drawstring casing.** Mark the placement of the casing on the top corners of the outer bag, on the wrong side. Starting at the left corner, make a mark ⅝" (1.5cm) down from the top of the bag, and then another mark below the first one, 1⅝" (4cm) down from the top of the bag. Draw a line connecting the marks, and then repeat this on the right corner. This space is where your drawstring will loop through your bag.

3 **Sew the outer bag.** Place the two outer bag pieces with right sides facing and align the edges. Sew along the sides and bottom of the outer bag piece, skipping over the marks you made for the drawstring casing in Step 2. Do not sew along the top edge so you can turn the bag right side out. Trim the seam allowances at the corners and turn right side out. Press your seams.

4 **Sew the lining.** Mark a 5" (12.5cm) line on the wrong side of a lining piece, centering it along the bottom edge. This marks your opening for turning. Place the lining pieces together with right sides facing and sew around the sides and bottom of the lining pieces like you did for the outer bag. Skip the marked line and the top edge. Trim the seam allowances at the corners and turn the lining right side out.

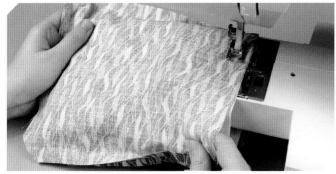

5 **Sew the top.** Nestle the lining into the outer bag with right sides facing. Align the top edges and sew all around the top edge to stitch the lining and outer fabric together. Turn the bag right side out through the opening in the lining and press it.

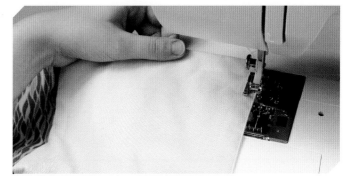

6 **Sew the opening closed.** Pull the lining out of the outer bag. Fold in the seam allowances around the opening in the lining, and machine sew close to the edge of the opening to close it.

Drawstring Ditty Bag *(continued)*

7 **Sew the drawstring casing.** Nestle the lining back into the outer bag and press the top seam. Mark a line 1" (2.5cm) down from the top edge of the top. Extend the line all the way around the top edge of the bag. Sew along this line to form the casing for your drawstring.

8 **Sew the drawstrings.** Fold the short ends of each of your drawstring pieces toward the wrong side by ⅝" (1.5cm). Then, fold each drawstring in half lengthwise with right sides together (so it's even skinnier) and sew along the raw edge. Turn the drawstrings right side out.

Turning Tubes

The idea of turning a tube inside out with just a safety pin sounds crazy, but it really works! Clip the safety pin to one end of the drawstring and begin feeding the pin through the tube. Continue feeding the pin through while pulling the tail of the tube back gently so as not to rip your fabric. When the safety pin emerges on the other end, pull the fabric entirely right side out and you're done! They make gadgets called fabric turners for doing this, but safety pins are always plentiful and cheap! Safety pins also replace another gadget called a bodkin, which works for what you'll be doing in Step 9.

Turning tubes: It's easy to turn tubes of fabric with just a safety pin. Just be sure to move slowly and carefully as you begin so you don't rip the fabric.

9 **Insert the drawstrings.** Attach a safety pin to the end of one drawstring. Starting with the safety pin, feed the drawstring into one of the casing holes near the top of the bag. Loop the drawstring through the casing the whole way around the bag, bringing the end back out on the same side that you started. Sew the two ends of your drawstrings together. Repeat this with the remaining drawstring, starting on the opposite side of the bag.

Drawstring Ditty Bag Patterns

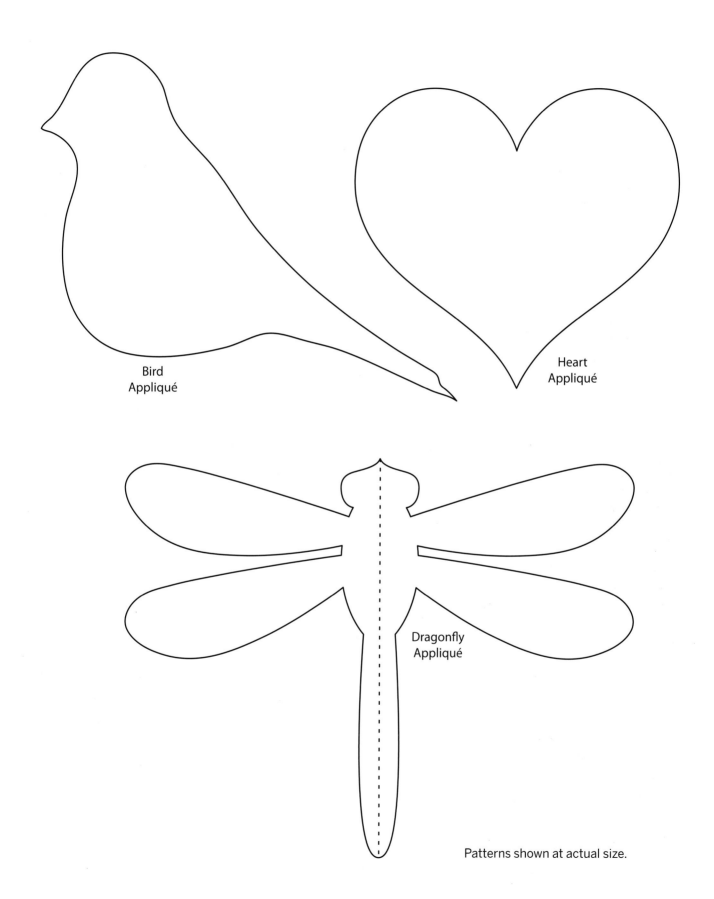

Bird
Appliqué

Heart
Appliqué

Dragonfly
Appliqué

Patterns shown at actual size.

Reversible Tote Bag

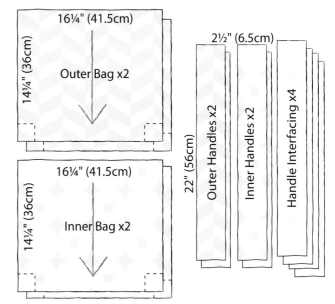

★★★☆☆☆☆☆

ESTIMATED TIME:
1–2 hours

TECHNIQUES:
Appliqué, Lining, Interfacing

MAKES:
One 12" x 12" (30.5 x 30.5cm) bag

This tote bag is the perfect little accessory for holding necessities, groceries, or even your newest fabric purchase. Not only that, it's reversible! Use adorable fabrics and the included apple, pear, square, circle, umbrella, and sun appliqué on the inside and outside and you'll have a bag that will fit whatever mood you're in.

Materials

- ☐ ⅔ yd. (67cm) of 45" (114.5cm)-wide or ½ yd. (50cm) of 60" (152.5cm)-wide light- to medium-weight woven fabric for outside

- ☐ ⅔ yd. (67cm) of 45" (114.5cm)-wide or ½ yd. (50cm) of 60" (152.5cm)-wide light- to medium-weight woven fabric for inside

- ☐ ¼ yd. (25cm) of 22" (56cm)-wide or ⅛ yd. (12.5cm) of 45" (114.5cm)-wide lightweight fusible interfacing

- ☐ Fat quarter of appliqué fabric (optional)

- ☐ ½ yd. (50cm) of fusible web (optional)

Tools

- ☐ Basic sewing kit (see page 25)

Your collection of fabric pieces for this project should look something like this:

16¼" (41.5cm)
14¼" (36cm)
Outer Bag x2

16¼" (41.5cm)
14¼" (36cm)
Inner Bag x2

2½" (6.5cm)
22" (56cm)
Outer Handles x2
Inner Handles x2
Handle Interfacing x4

THE PREP WORK:

Cut your fabric pieces using the following chart. Cut any additional appliqué pieces from the patterns on page 82.

Reversible Tote Bag Pieces

Piece Name	Material to Cut	Size to Cut	Number to Cut	Seam Allowance
Outer Bag	Light- to medium-weight woven	16¼" x 14¼" (41.5 x 36cm)	2	⅝" (1.5cm)
Inner Bag	Light- to medium-weight woven	16¼" x 14¼" (41.5 x 36cm)	2	⅝" (1.5cm)
Outer Handles	Outer bag fabric	2½" x 22" (6.5 x 56cm)	2	⅝" (1.5cm)
Inner Handles	Inner bag fabric	2½" x 22" (6.5 x 56cm)	2	⅝" (1.5cm)
Handle Interfacing	Lightweight interfacing	2½" x 22" (6.5 x 56cm)	4	⅝" (1.5cm)

Reversible Tote Bag *(continued)*

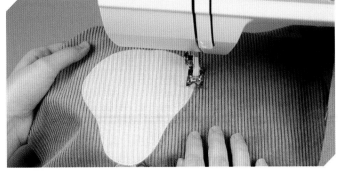

1 **Appliqué your design (optional).** See the Getting Started chapter (page 37) to choose a method for applying your decorative fabric to the outer/inner bag. Sew your appliqué in the center of the bag pieces, or at least 1" (2.5cm) down from the top and 3" (7.5cm) in from either side or the bottom.

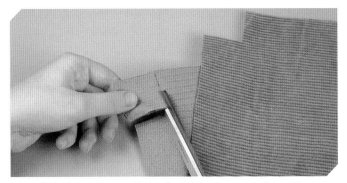

2 **Cut the corners.** Cut a 1½" (4cm) square from the bottom left and right corners of all inner and outer bag pieces.

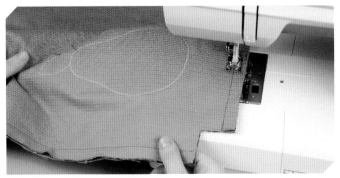

3 **Sew the bag sides.** Align the two outer bag pieces with right sides together. Sew along the sides and bottom, skipping over the corners and the top edge. Repeat with the two inner bag pieces.

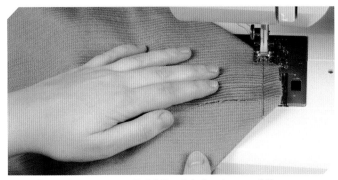

4 **Sew the corners.** Fold the fabric at one of the corners of the outer bag at a 45° angle, causing the side and bottom seams to match up and the raw edges to align. Sew straight across this corner to create depth for the bag. Repeat with the remaining outer bag corner and the two corners for the inner bag.

5 **Apply the interfacing.** Place one of the handle interfacing pieces over one of the handle pieces, lining up the edges. Following the manufacturer's directions, fuse the interfacing completely to the wrong side of the fabric. Repeat with the remaining interfacing and the inner and outer handle pieces.

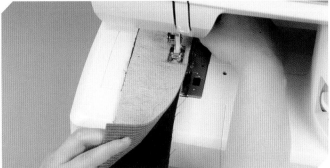

6 **Sew the handle halves.** Match up an outer handle piece with an inner handle piece with right sides facing. Sew them together along one of the long edges. Press the seam open. Repeat with the remaining two handle pieces.

Reversible Tote Bag (continued)

7 **Complete the handles.** Fold over each long edge of a handle toward the wrong side by ⅝" (1.5cm). Iron the folds in place. Then, fold the entire handle in half lengthwise along the seam, with wrong sides together. Iron the fold in place. Topstitch along each long edge of the handle to secure the folds. Repeat with the second handle.

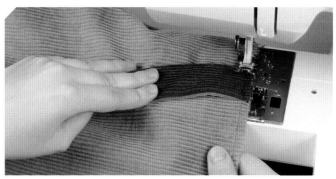

8 **Baste the handles.** Working on the wrong side of the outer bag, find and mark the center of the top edge of the front and back of the bag. From this point, measure out 3" (7.5cm) to each side and trace the outline of the end of a handle there. This marks the placement of your handles. Using the marks as a guide, baste the handle ends to the top edge of the bag within the seam allowances. Make sure the handle ends are pointing toward the top of the bag as shown when you baste them in place.

9 **Sew the top.** Nestle the outer bag into the inner bag with right sides facing. Using a side seam as a center point, mark a 5" (12.5cm) line along the top edge of the bag. This marks your opening for turning. Pin the bag pieces together along the top edge. Sew around the top edge, skipping over the marked line.

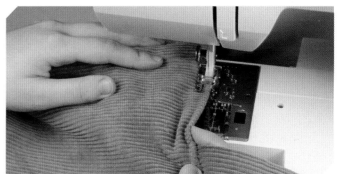

10 **Sew the opening closed.** Turn the bag right side out and fold in the seam allowances around the opening in the top edge. Press all of the bag's seams and particularly the folds around the opening. Sew along the outside top edge of the bag again, stitching ⅛" (0.5cm) from the edge. This will sew the opening closed.

Design your own!

Did you enjoy drafting your own patterns for the Book Cover (page 50)? Then know that making your own custom-sized tote bag is also within your reach! Decide on the dimensions you'd like for your bag and add 4¼" (11cm) to the width measurement and 2¾" (7cm) to the length measurement. Follow the rest of the directions as before!

Reversible Tote Bag Patterns

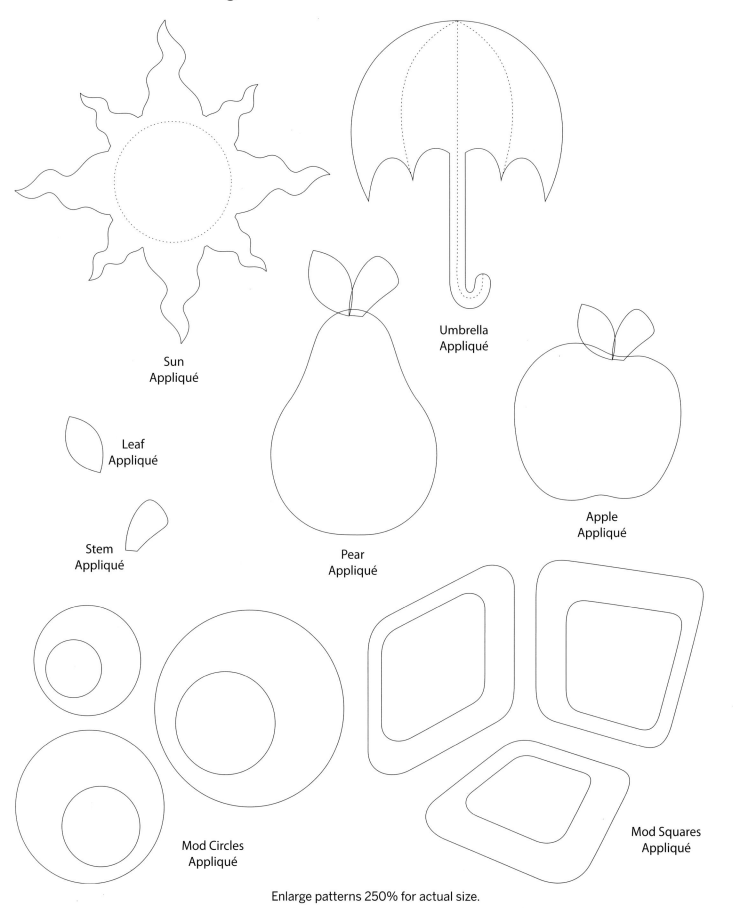

Sun
Appliqué

Umbrella
Appliqué

Leaf
Appliqué

Apple
Appliqué

Stem
Appliqué

Pear
Appliqué

Mod Circles
Appliqué

Mod Squares
Appliqué

Enlarge patterns 250% for actual size.

Mini Messenger Bag

★★★☆☆☆☆☆

⏱ **ESTIMATED TIME:**
45–90 minutes

⚙ **TECHNIQUES:**
Appliqué, Lining, Interfacing,
Hook-and-Loop Tape

✓ **MAKES:**
One 8 ½" x 9 ½" (21.5 x 24cm) bag

This all-purpose bag is great as a casual purse or errand bag. The handy front pockets can hold little items and the hook-and-loop flap with additional record adapter, starburst, and squid appliqué designs keeps it all safely tucked away!

Materials

- ☐ ½ yd. (50cm) of light- to medium-weight woven fabric for outside
- ☐ ½ yd. (50cm) of lightweight woven fabric for lining
- ☐ ¼ yd. (25cm) of lightweight fusible interfacing
- ☐ 2" (5cm) of hook-and-loop tape
- ☐ Fat quarter or 6" x 6" (15 x 15cm) scrap of appliqué fabric (optional)
- ☐ 6" x 6" (15 x 15cm) square of fusible web (optional)

Tools

- ☐ Basic sewing kit (see page 25)
- ☒ Chopstick or similar turning tool

Your collection of fabric pieces for this project should look something like this:

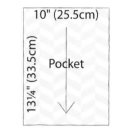

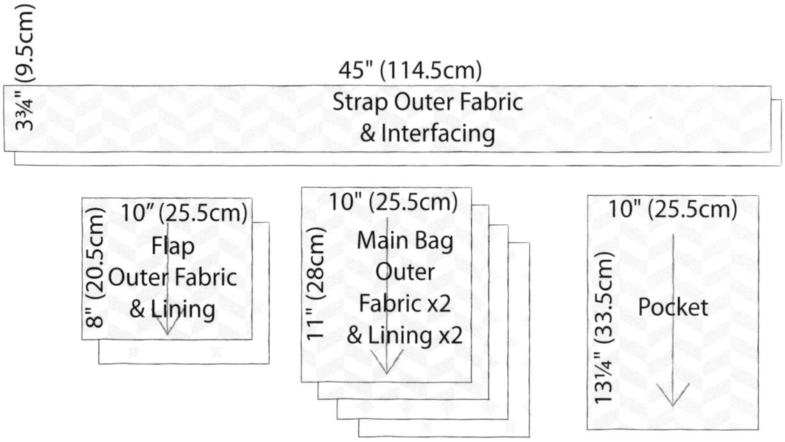

3¾" (9.5cm)

45" (114.5cm)
Strap Outer Fabric & Interfacing

8" (20.5cm) / 10" (25.5cm)
Flap Outer Fabric & Lining

11" (28cm) / 10" (25.5cm)
Main Bag Outer Fabric x2 & Lining x2

13¼" (33.5cm) / 10" (25.5cm)
Pocket

THE PREP WORK:

Cut your fabric pieces using the following chart. Cut any additional appliqué pieces from the patterns on page 87.

Mini Messenger Bag Pieces

Piece Name	Material to Cut	Size to Cut	Number to Cut	Seam Allowance
Main Bag Outer Fabric	Light- to medium-weight woven	10" x 11" (25.5 x 28cm)	2	⅝" (1.5cm)
Main Bag Lining	Lightweight woven	10" x 11" (25.5 x 28cm)	2	⅝" (1.5cm)
Pocket	Light- to medium-weight woven	10" x 13¼" (25.5 x 33.5cm)	1	⅝" (1.5cm)
Flap Outer Fabric	Light- to medium-weight woven	10" x 8" (23 x 20.5cm)	1	⅝" (1.5cm)
Flap Lining	Lightweight woven	10" x 8" (25.5 x 20.5cm)	1	⅝" (1.5cm)
Strap Outer Fabric	Light- to medium-weight woven	3¾" x 45" (9.5 x 114.5cm)	1	⅝" (1.5cm)
Strap Interfacing	Lightweight interfacing	3¾" x 45" (9.5 x 114.5cm)	1	⅝" (1.5cm)

Mini Messenger Bag *(continued)*

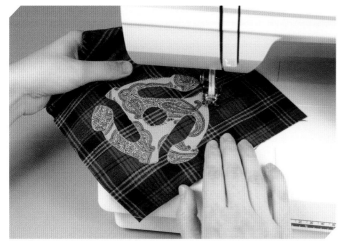

1 **Appliqué your design (optional).** See the Getting Started chapter (page 37) to choose a method for applying your decorative fabric to the flap front. Sew your appliqué in the center of the flap front, or at least 1" (2.5cm) in from the edge.

2 **Apply the hook-and-loop tape.** Fold the pocket piece in half widthwise with wrong sides together, aligning the edges. Position the loop side of the hook-and-loop tape on the pocket 5" (12.5cm) up from the bottom edge (the open side opposite the fold). Center the hook-and-loop tape on the pocket. Position the hook side of the hook-and-loop tape on the right side of the flap lining, 1" (2.5cm) from the bottom edge and centered. Sew the hook-and-loop tape pieces in place.

3 **Baste the pocket.** Place the pocket on the right side of the outer bag front piece, lining up the bottom edges. Make sure the folded edge of the pocket is at the top and the hook and loop tape is facing out. Baste the pocket in place by sewing along the bottom and sides within the seam allowances. Mark a dividing line on the pocket front, going vertically down the center (about 5" [12.5cm] in from each side). Sew along this line to create two sections in the pocket.

4 **Sew the main bag.** Layer the outer bag pieces together with right sides facing, matching up the raw edges. Sew along the sides and the bottom, leaving the top open for turning right side out. Trim the seam allowances and press the seams.

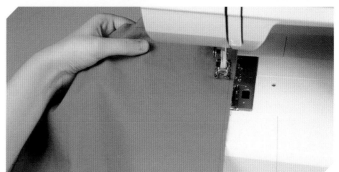

5 **Sew the lining.** Mark a 5" (12.5cm) line on the wrong side of one of the lining pieces, centering it along the bottom edge. This marks the opening for turning. Layer the lining pieces together with right sides facing, and sew along the sides and bottom as you did for the outer bag pieces in Step 4, but skip over the marked line and the top edge. Trim the seam allowances, and press the seams.

Mini Messenger Bag (continued)

6 **Sew the flap.** Layer the outer flap and flap lining pieces together with right sides facing. Sew along the sides and bottom, leaving the top open for turning right side out. Trim the seam allowances, turn the flap right side out, and press it.

7 **Apply the interfacing.** Place the strap interfacing over the strap piece, lining up the edges. Following the manufacturer's directions, fuse the interfacing completely to the wrong side of the fabric.

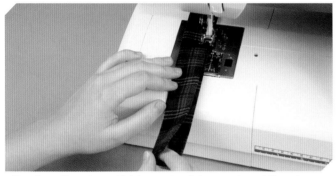

8 **Sew the strap.** Fold over each long edge of the strap toward the wrong side by ⅝" (1.5cm). Iron the folds in place. Fold the entire strap in half lengthwise with wrong sides together. Iron the fold in place. Sew along the open long edge of the strap to form a tube.

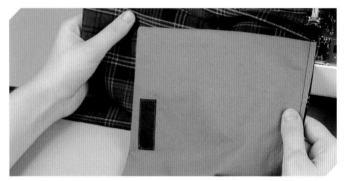

9 **Baste the strap and flap.** Center each end of the strap over a side seam of the outer bag with right sides together. Make sure the strap is not twisted and the strap ends are pointing toward the top edge of the bag. Line up the open edge of the flap piece with the top back edge of the outer bag, right sides together. Baste all of these pieces in place by sewing along the top edge of the outer bag within the seam allowances.

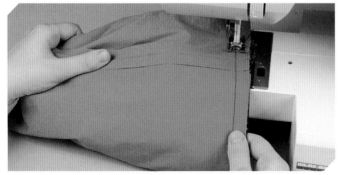

10 **Sew the bag top.** Nestle the outer bag into the lining with right sides facing, aligning the top raw edges. Sew along the entire top edge, stitching through the straps and flap as well as the outer bag fabric and lining.

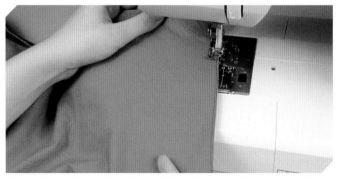

11 **Sew the lining closed.** Turn the bag right side out through the opening in the lining. Press the top edge of the bag. Fold in the seam allowances around the opening in the lining and sew it closed with a ladder stitch or machine stitch.

Mini Messenger Bag Patterns

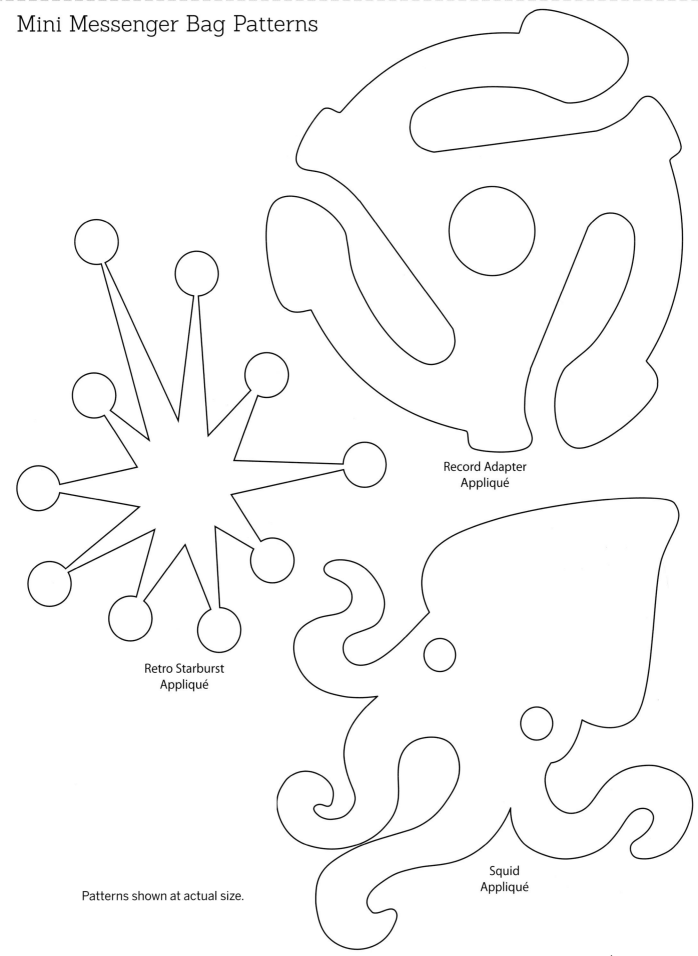

Record Adapter
Appliqué

Retro Starburst
Appliqué

Squid
Appliqué

Patterns shown at actual size.

Polished Ruffled Purse

★★★★★★★☆☆

⏱ **ESTIMATED TIME:**
1–2 hours

TECHNIQUES:
Gathering, Interfacing, Snaps, Lining

✓ **MAKES:**
One 10" x 7" (25.5 x 18cm) purse

This pretty little purse works great as both casual wear and elegant wear. Pair it either with jeans or a little black dress for a very stylish look. It has such an adorable shape, you won't believe it's made from such simple pieces! Keep the style simple by using a sew-in snap, or find a decorative snap for a fun or elegant look.

Materials

☐ ½ yd. (50cm) of lightweight woven fabric for outer bag

☐ ½ yd. (50cm) of lightweight woven fabric for lining

☐ ¼ yd. (25cm) of lightweight interfacing

☐ One sew-in or metal prong snap, ¼" to ¾" (0.5 to 2cm) in diameter

Tools

☐ Basic sewing kit (see page 25)

☐ Snap installing tools (if applicable)

Your collection of fabric pieces for this project should look something like this:

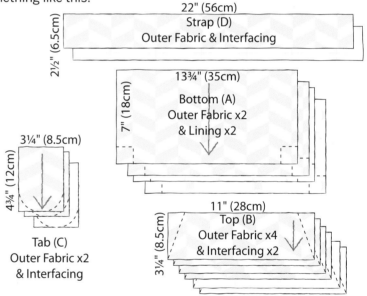

THE PREP WORK:

Cut your fabric pieces using the following chart.

Polished Ruffled Purse Pieces

Piece Name	Material to Cut	Size to Cut	Number to Cut	Seam Allowance
Bottom (A) Outer Fabric	Lightweight woven	13¾" x 7" (35 x 18cm)	2	⅝" (1.5cm)
Bottom (A) Lining	Lightweight woven	13¾" x 7" (35 x 18cm)	2	⅝" (1.5cm)
Top (B) Outer Fabric	Lightweight woven	11" x 3¼" (28 x 8.5cm)	4	⅝" (1.5cm)
Top (B) Interfacing	Lightweight interfacing	11" x 3¼" (28 x 8.5cm)	2	⅝" (1.5cm)
Tab (C) Outer Fabric	Lightweight woven	3¼" x 4¾" (8.5 x 12cm)	2	⅝" (1.5cm)
Tab (C) Interfacing	Lightweight interfacing	3¼" x 4¾" (8.5 x 12cm)	1	⅝" (1.5cm)
Strap (D) Outer Fabric	Lightweight woven	22" x 2½" (56 x 6.5cm)	1	⅝" (1.5cm)
Strap (D) Interfacing	Lightweight interfacing	22" x 2½" (56 x 6.5cm)	1	⅝" (1.5cm)

Polished Ruffled Purse (continued)

1 **Apply the interfacing.** Place the interfacing pieces over their corresponding fabric pieces (B, C, and D), lining up the edges. Following the manufacturer's directions, fuse the interfacing pieces completely to the wrong sides of the fabric pieces.

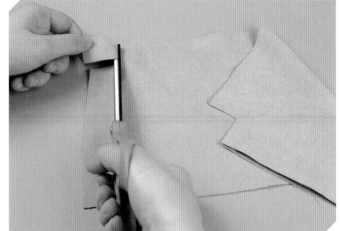

2 **Trim the fabric.** Cut 1¼" (3cm) squares from the bottom corners of the purse bottom pieces (A) in both the outer fabric and the lining. Trace the curve of a soup can or cup onto one short end of each tab piece (C). Trim the fabric along the line to create a tab with a rounded end. Measure 1" (2.5cm) in from each short end along the top edge of the purse top (B). Draw a line from the bottom corner to this point and trim along this line to create a trapezoid. Reference the dotted lines on the illustrations on page 88 for help with this step.

3 **Gather the purse bottom.** Sew two parallel lines of straight stitches at the longest length possible along the top edge of each of the four purse bottom pieces (A). Sew the two lines of stitches within the seam allowances. Once the stitches are complete, pull on the bobbin threads to gather the fabric (see page 34). Gather the fabric until it is about 10½" (26.5cm) wide.

4 **Sew the top.** Match up the bottom edge of an interfaced purse top piece (B) with the top gathered edge of a purse bottom piece (A) with right sides facing. The raw edges along the sides shouldn't match up, but the seam lines should. Draw them in with a fabric marker if it helps to see this. If desired, you can always take in more gathers, or let out gathers to make the side edges match up. Sew along the gathered edge, and then press the seam. Repeat this to join the remaining three purse bottom pieces with the remaining three purse top pieces.

Polished Ruffled Purse *(continued)*

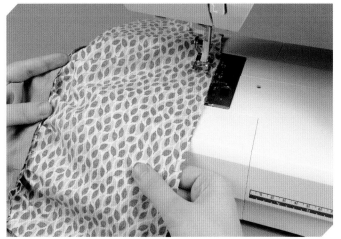

5 **Sew the sides and bottom.** Match up the raw edges of the sides and bottom of the two lining pieces with right sides facing. Do the same with the outer bag pieces. Mark a 5" (12.5cm) line on the wrong side of the lining, centering it along the bottom edge. This marks the opening for turning. Sew along the sides and bottom of the outer fabric and then the lining pieces, leaving the top edges free, and skipping over the line marked on the lining. Press the seams.

6 **Sew the corners.** Fold the fabric at one corner of the lining bottom (A) at a 45° angle, causing the side and bottom seams to match up and the raw edges to align. Sew straight across this edge to shape the corner. Repeat with the remaining lining corner and the outer bag corners.

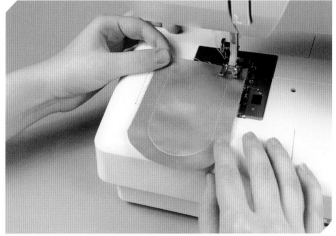

7 **Sew the tab.** Match up the tab pieces (C) with right sides facing and sew along the sides and rounded edge, leaving the top straight edge open for turning right side out. Notch the seam allowances, turn the tab right side out, and press the seam.

8 **Sew the straps.** Fold over each long edge of the strap toward the wrong side by ⅝" (1.5cm). Iron the folds in place. Fold the entire strap in half lengthwise with wrong sides together, and iron the fold in place. Sew the strap closed along the open long edge to form a tube.

Polished Ruffled Purse (continued)

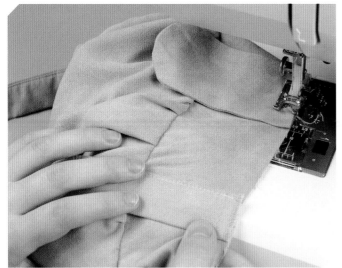

9 **Baste the straps and tab.** Center each end of the strap over a side seam of the outer bag with right sides together. Make sure the strap is not twisted and the strap ends are pointing toward the top edge of the bag. Center the straight edge of the tab along the top edge of the back of the bag. Baste the tab and strap ends in place by sewing along the top edge of the outer bag, within the seam allowances.

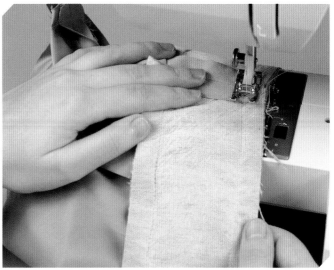

10 **Sew the purse top.** Nestle the lining into the outer bag with right sides together, matching up the top edges and pinning them in place. Sew completely around the top edge.

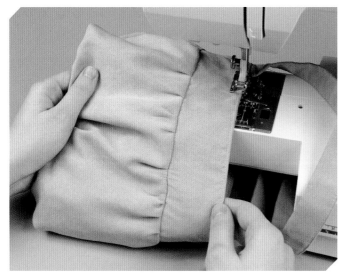

11 **Complete the purse.** Turn the purse right side out through the opening in the lining. Press the top seam and edge stitch around it. Fold in the seam allowances around the opening in the lining and hand or machine sew the opening closed.

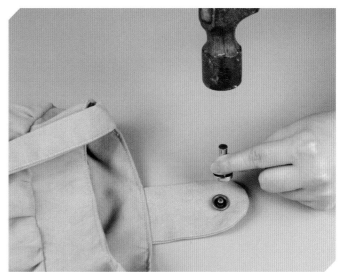

12 **Install the snaps.** If using metal prong snaps, install the socket half in the middle the purse top that is opposite the tab. Install the stud half in the center of the tab, about ⅝" (1.5cm) from the rounded edge. Follow the instructions on page 93 for installing the snaps.

Installing Snaps

Snaps are another great closure to tie up your latest project. The sew-in variety is extremely dainty and unobtrusive—perfect if you want a completely inconspicuous closure. If you go with the prong variety, they look quite classy and have a much stronger hold than hook-and-loop tape.

Varieties of snaps: Sew-in snaps vary in size from very dainty sizes at ¼" (0.5cm) in diameter up to large 1" (2.5cm)-diameter sizes. Prong snaps are typically made from various colors of metal but can also vary in size. The actual cap of the snap can be decorative or plain, but the construction is almost always the same.

Setting sew-in snaps: Sew-in snaps typically have several holes on the sides that allow you to anchor the snap to your project with your thread. Place the stud end of your snap on the part of the project that will be facing downward, where the pattern indicates. Sew it in place and prepare to sew the socket piece.

You can mark the end of the stud with your fabric marker or a bit of chalk, and then rub the stud onto the fabric of your project. This is where you can install your socket piece. The pattern may also indicate where to sew your snap socket, but this can serve as an insurance policy. Repeat the same process for sewing the socket part of the snap as you did for the stud.

Setting prong snaps: Prong snaps are much stronger than sew-in snaps because they're held together with hooked metal. Your fabric should be reinforced with interfacing whenever possible if you'll be installing prong snaps.

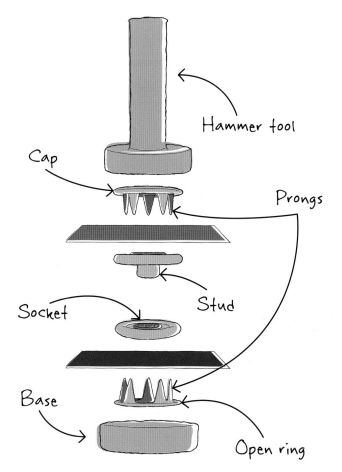

Hammer tool

Cap

Prongs

Stud

Socket

Base

Open ring

Anatomy of a snap: To ensure proper installation, prong snaps should be hammered in a specific order.

Varieties of snaps: Snaps come in sew-in varieties and prong varieties that are installed with a hammer.

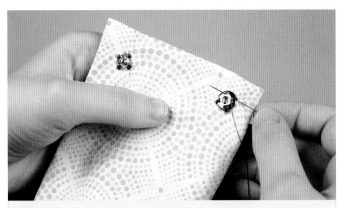

Sew-in snaps: Anchor the sew-in snaps to your project with several stitches around the holes in the snap—about three to five. Slip the needle between the layers of the fabric toward the next hole and repeat the process until you've sewn all the way around.

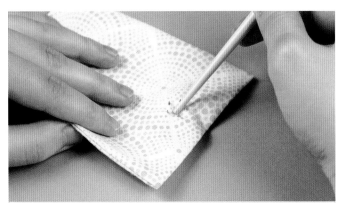

Prong snaps: Insert the snap cap. Find and mark the area where the snap needs to be installed. From the underside, poke the prongs through the fabric so they're visible on the other side. Use a pencil or similar tool to poke into the center and force the prongs to come through.

Completing the snap: When you've finished hammering your prong snap, be sure that the pieces have no space between them and are completely joined. If you pull at it lightly, the snap should not give. If the join isn't strong, it's best to pull the snaps apart with pliers, straighten out the prongs, and try again. Repeat this same process with the snap ring that serves as the next prong piece plus the socket piece. This part should be installed on your project so the ring faces inward.

Troubleshooting: Sometimes no matter what you try, you can't get the prongs to make a strong enough join. Perhaps when the snap is closed you can't open it again without ripping it out of the fabric. I've had this issue many times before, and this can result from the stud and socket being off in size by a bit. To solve this problem, I found that putting a dab of multi-purpose craft glue on your fabric before setting the snap works wonders. You must make sure the glue dries completely before you attempt to open and close the snap again, but it's a great insurance policy against snaps that are too tight!

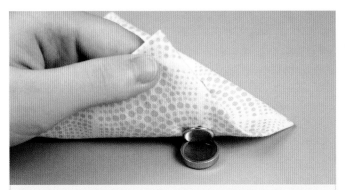

Prong snaps: Rest the snap cap. Nestle the cap onto your setting tool. You should feel it rest there easily so that it won't move while it's hammered.

Prong snaps: Hammer the snap. Set the snap socket piece on top of the prongs. You should feel it rest in the grooves. When you know that it feels settled, set your hammering tool on top of the socket and hammer it well. When the snap is hammered, the prongs of the snap cap are forced backward and into the grooves of the socket when the hammer tool strikes them.

Quick Reference Chart

		Fabric	Pros	Cons	Applications	Other names/ similar fabrics
Wovens	**Lightweight**	Quilting cotton	Sews easily, forgiving	Sometimes stiff	Bedclothes, bags, shirts, skirts, pajamas, dresses	Broadcloth, sateen, voile, lawn
		Flannel	Soft, sews easily	Tends to pill	Bedclothes, pajamas	Plaid shirting, flannel-backed satin
		Shirting	Crisp, textured	Less breathable	Shirts, dresses, belts & similar accessories	Gingham, seersucker, crepe, poplin
		Satin	Smooth, drapey	Slippery, delicate	Dresses, tops, skirts	Charmeuse, dupioni, chiffon
	Medium-weight	Linen	Drapey, textured	Unravels easily	Shirts, dresses, skirts, bags	Suiting fabric, wool, rayon
		Twill	Crisp, sews easily	Less forgiving	Slacks, skirts, light jackets, bags, accessories	Bottomweights, denim, sateen twill
		Corduroy	Soft, crisp, sews easily	Distinctive nap	Skirts, light jackets, bags, accessories	Thin chenille, embossed fabrics
		Brocade	Lustrous, crisp	Unravels easily, not forgiving	Skirts, light jackets, bags, accessories, belts, dresses	Bridal satin, taffeta, sari fabric
	Heavyweight	Canvas	Dense, strong, crisp	Not forgiving	Bags, belts, accessories	Cotton duck, burlap
		Home décor fabrics	Dense, strong, crisp	Not forgiving	Bags, belts, accessories	Upholstery fabric, printed twill, canvas
		Faux suede	Soft, crisp, sews easily	Doesn't iron well	Skirts, jackets, bags, accessories, belts	Suedecloth, ultrasuede
Knits	**Lightweight**	Jersey	Drapey, soft	Stretches while sewing	T-shirts, skirts, dresses, activewear	Single knit, thermal knit
		Lycra	Drapey, four-way stretch	Stretches while sewing	T-shirts, skirts, dresses, activewear, bathing suits	Tricot, spandex, nylon knit, rayon knit
	Medium-weight	Interlock	Stable, breatheable	Less stretch, less drape	T-shirts, skirts, dresses, activewear, accessories	Double knit, rib knit, sweater knit
		Fleece	Stable, soft, forgiving	Less stretch, tends to pill	Jackets, hats, plush toys, accessories	Sweatshirt knit, microfleece, minky

Index

Note: Page numbers in *italics* indicate projects/patterns.